CAUTION:
Christians Under Construction

A nuts and bolts look at living a not-so-perfect Christian life

by Bill Hybels
with Jay Caress

This book is designed for your personal reading pleasure and profit. It is also designed for group study. A leader's guide, with visual aids (SonPower Multiuse Transparency Masters) is available from your local Christian bookstore or from the publisher.

VICTOR BOOKS

a division of SP Publications, Inc., Wheaton, Illinois
Offices also in Fullerton, California • Whitby, Ontario, Canada • London, England

PROPERTY OF CHRISTIAN EDUCATION DEPARTMENT

Bible quotations are from the *New American Standard Bible* (NASB), © 1960, 1962, 1963, 1968, 1971, 1972, 1973, The Lockman Foundation, La Habra, California; the *New International Version* (NIV), © 1973 by New York Bible Society International, published by the Zondervan Publishing House; and *The Living Bible* (LB), © 1971 by Tyndale House Publishers, Wheaton, Illinois.

Library of Congress Catalog Card Number: 77-93854
ISBN: 0-88207-759-7

VICTOR BOOKS
A division of SP Publications, Inc.
P.O. Box 1825 ● Wheaton, Ill. 60187

Contents

1
Misconceptions of Christianity

I got off a plane in Los Angeles not long ago and as I was walking through the airport, a young man with a Bible in his hand began to talk to me.

"Do you have anything troubling you? Are there problems in your life?" he asked.

Then before I could answer him, he looked me in the eye and said, "Jesus can take all your troubles away!"

Sounds a little extreme, I thought. He continued, "Really! You'll never have problems again. Jesus can take them all away. Everything can be bliss with Him in your life!"

I had the feeling I'd heard this type of presentation before, but it wasn't until later that I remembered where—in a used car lot!

A salesman had praised a particular car and said, "This car will never need a thing. It won't need spark plugs. It won't need oil changes. *This car will never give you a problem.*"

Next I thought he'd tell me the car would run on water instead of gasoline. This man was insulting my intelligence. *All* cars need some kind of maintenance sooner or later—whom was he trying to kid?

What's true of cars is also true of life. Instinctively and by experience we know there will always be some problems in life. So when someone says, "Jesus will take all your problems away," we know it's an unrealistic statement.

Yet some people become Christians, turn their lives over to Jesus Christ, and carry this "no problems" idea in the backs of their minds. Then when difficulties come up, they really get down on themselves, because "Christians aren't supposed to have such problems."

A youth director I know had been a Christian about two or three years when he began to experience loneliness. He felt very ashamed of this emptiness in his life.

Meanwhile, in his role as a counselor, he caught himself trying to convince high school students that with Jesus they would never to be lonely. It bothered him that he wasn't experiencing what he taught.

Many of us have similar dilemmas. We try to take on a false image of maturity and growth in the Lord and we refuse to admit that we have our downs as well as our ups.

This causes two problems. First, we Christians get depressed and defeated because these hassles "aren't supposed to happen."

Secondly, people who aren't Christians observe that we're living in a fantasy world. They can see we have problems, and if we won't admit it, they correctly assume that we are living in self-deception. How can we expect them to believe this gospel of "trouble-free bliss" when we have very visible hang-ups in our own lives?

Misconception Number 1:
Christianity Is "Trouble-Free"

The sad part of the story about the car salesman is that *he turned me away from what might have been a very good car.* And we may turn people away from Jesus Christ when we make misleading claims about Him.

Let's get this straight: God does not guarantee anywhere in the Bible that Christians will live trouble-free lives. On the contrary, there's a high probability that as a Christian, you'll have problems that you've never faced before.

When you're not a Christian, you live pretty much to please yourself. You do what you want to do and go where you want to go. If someone wrongs you, you're free to hate him. Who's telling you not to?

But when you become a Christian, God puts His Spirit inside you and suddenly you begin to see the needs of people around you. That can cause some pain. Other people's problems become *your* problems, because you care.

If a friend or a member of your family has a problem or some kind of personal tragedy, it shoots a deep pang of sadness into your life. God has made you more sensitive, and that means you're more vulnerable now.

So if you're considering Christianity or if you're trying to live it out, don't expect your Christian life to be a life of perfect bliss. The uniqueness of our Christian lives is not that they are always problem-free, but that we have Someone who can provide supernatural help for us.

Jesus told His disciples, "Here on earth you will have many trials and sorrows; but cheer up, for I have overcome the world" (John 16:33, LB).

There will be problems in our lives; there will be tragedies. But as the Apostle John says, "greater is He who is in you than he who is in the world" (1 John 4:4, NASB). This means God can give you the inner strength to *deal* with the problems in your life—whatever they might be.

So if you're trying to tell people about Jesus Christ, don't mislead them. There will be *difficulties*. The difference is that God promises to help us cope with them.

Misconception Number 2:
Christianity Is Easy

Another misconception that people propagate about Christianity is related to the preceding one. Stated simply it is this: *Christianity is easy.*

Have you ever heard a Christian make a statement like this? "I always feel love for everyone. It's easy for me. I give a quarter of my income to the Lord. It's a breeze to do it. It's easy for me to face my troubles with an attitude of peace."

Baloney.

Now, it may be true that *becoming* a Christian is relatively easy. If you're willing to let Jesus Christ come into your life and be your Forgiver, your Friend, and your Controller, then God's gift of a new life in Christ is free—it's yours for the asking.

But no way is it easy to live a continuously committed Christian life. Living out a vital Christian life is a cooperative effort involving your will and God's power. God helps you lead the Christian life, but you have to cooperate with Him—and obeying Him isn't always a piece of cake.

Let's take the area of love. Many people make the statement that "God can fill your heart with love so that you can love everybody." In a sense that may be true, but sometimes it isn't easy to apply.

For example, I love my wife more than anyone else in the world, and usually it's not too hard to show that love. But when she was pregnant with our daughter, she did a lot of things that didn't seem to fit her personality at all, and sometimes I had a problem loving her.

One night during this time, I came home dead tired. I was exhausted. About 3 o'clock in the morning, after some fitful sleep, my wife woke me up and said, "I want a bowl of soup."

Are you kidding? I thought. Obviously I didn't feel an overwhelming surge of love for her right at that moment, and I came pretty close to letting it show. But she *was* pregnant, and she *was* sick, and it was *our* baby. So I said, "All right. OK." And I got up and sleepily fixed her a can of soup and brought it to her in a bowl with a big spoon.

"Where are the crackers?" she asked.

"Crackers! Crackers!?" I said. I was thinking, *I'll get you crackers, all right.* But I dutifully got her some crackers.

This may seem like a rather humorous, petty example, but it illustrates my point. It's not always easy to behave in a loving way, but we still have to do it. God says to love even when it's difficult.

Secondly, the Christian life is not easy when it comes to decision-making. A person who is not a Christian has a simple pattern to follow. He says, "This is what I want to do; this is where I want to go," and so on.

But when you become a Christian, God wants to have a part in your decision-making process. All of a sudden, you can't just do whatever you want. You can't just make snap decisions. God says, "I want to help so you won't make the wrong decisions."

It's really tough sometimes. Take the area of morality. Who legislates your morals if you're not a Christian? Most likely *you* do. But after you know Jesus Christ, you begin to follow the biblical patterns. And they're not always easy to follow.

The Bible says, "Those who do what God says—they are living with God and He with them" (1 John 3:24, LB). Think of all that implies! It means unselfish love, self-control, and single-minded devotion to God.

If someone tells you that all of this is easy, don't believe him. It's not. Living a successful Christian life is possible and it can be done joyfully with God's help—but it'll never be easy.

Misconception Number 3:
Christianity Is Confining

A third misconception people have about Christianity is that it's terribly *confining*. This is what I thought for many years.

I attended a small Christian college in Iowa for two years, where I majored in business administration. I lived with some friends in a big house off campus, but we often ate our meals in the college cafeteria. In that large room, there was one group of students you could always pick out of the 1,000 or so students.

They were the preseminarians—the close-knit group of guys who were going into "full-time Christian service." Most of them would become pastors. Somehow they always stood apart from the crowd.

For example, each fall the physical education staff sponsored intramural touch football tournaments. Everyone would wear grubbies—no uniforms required. So we'd all put on jeans and sweatshirts—everyone except the "presemers." They still wore their slick black pants.

They also never wanted to play tackle. And when we were done, they never took showers with the rest of us.

Naturally I began to get the idea if a person was going to be a serious Christian, he had to be a real "loser." I thought I'd have to look just right and act just so. I thought I'd have to conform to the standards of the preseminarians if I ever really gave my life to Jesus Christ.

To me Christianity meant obeying a set of confining rules and developing a carefully regimented life-style like all the other look-alikes. I wasn't interested.

Then one day I heard a statement that turned my life around: "Christianity is not obeying a set of rules; it is a relationship with a living person—Jesus Christ."

That made all the difference in the world. A Christian doesn't have to fall into step with a group of regimented look-alikes. A Christian can develop his personality in his own unique way under God's personal direction. He can be as "normal" as anybody else. There is no verse of Scripture to back up the misconception that one has to be strange to be a sold-out Christian.

Jesus never talked about stamping us out like mannequins in a factory. He said, "If therefore the Son shall make you free, you shall be free indeed" (John 8:36, NASB).

Jesus was saying, "If you want to be free from the pressures of living and the downward cycle of your own desires, I can set you free like you've never been before."

Freedom is not found in avoiding Jesus Christ; freedom is in losing yourself in Him. Jesus Christ can give you an inner freedom that you can express in your own unique way.

The Bible talks about how to set up a church. In essence it says, "Don't all of you try to do the same thing. Everybody's not destined to be a pastor. There are all kinds of unique ways to serve the Lord and to serve each other" (see 1 Corinthians 12:27-31).

Christianity isn't a profession. There should be people from all walks of life taking Jesus Christ with them into their unique spheres of influence. Christianity isn't a strict dress code or a way of talking or any kind of box that people have to squeeze into. It's a living relationship with Jesus Christ.

Misconception Number 4: Christianity Is Boring

The fourth misconception that many people hold about Christianity is that it's *boring*.

They think all the *real* action is in the business world, or in sports, or in a so-called unconventional life-style.

However, if you begin to look at the lives of the characters in the Bible, you don't exactly find a bunch of weak-willed milktoasts sitting around a tea-table. Moses, for example, had more hair-raising adventures than most of us could *dream* of in two lifetimes!

Abraham, David, the Apostle Paul—they all led daring, adventurous, zestful, unconventional lives. And that's the way the Christian life is meant to be.

"What kind of adventure are you talking about?" you may ask.

I'm talking about the great adventure of seeing people's lives—including your own—dramatically changed, the adventure of finding you can serve God in a way that fits your personality perfectly and stretches your abilities to their fullest potential.

God can change the complexion of the world through you. If you're living a sold-out Christian life with the power of God's Spirit flowing through you, you can affect a lot of lives. You and the people you touch can bring hope, comfort, encouragement, and truth to a great number of people who are hurting and who desperately need what only Jesus Christ can give.

This knowledge, that my life has made a positive difference in other people's lives, and that these people influence still others, has given me a tremendous sense of satisfaction. There's adventure in knowing that your life is *worth something* in God's eternal plan. Christianity when it's lived authentically is the farthest thing from boredom that I can imagine.

Misconception Number 5:
Becoming a Christian Means . . .

Finally, the biggest misconception about Christianity may be in how one *becomes* a Christian. If you'd walk out on a busy street and ask ten people, you'd probably get ten different answers.

Everybody thinks he knows the answer. People say you can become a Christian by joining a church or by having good intentions or by such a simple thing as being an American citizen.

Sometimes I wonder where people are getting their information. Do we have the right to just dream up how we think a person becomes a Christian? Or is there an authoritative answer to this question?

In the Book of John, the Bible tells about a man named Nicodemus who came to Jesus with a deep spiritual hunger. Jesus told him, "Unless one is *born again,* he cannot see the kingdom of God" (John 3:3, NASB).

Nicodemus didn't exactly understand what Jesus was talking about. He asked, "How can a man be born again when he is old? He cannot enter a second time into his mother's womb and be born, can he?" (John 3:4, NASB)

Jesus answered him by telling him, in effect, "The first time you were born, you were born in a physical way into a physical family. The second time, you come to Me and I put My Spirit within you and you're reborn into the spiritual family of God. It's a *spiritual* rebirth" (John 1:12; 3:6).

It is that spiritual rebirth, the experience of

being "born again" into the family of God that makes a person a Christian. If there has never been a point in your life when you have been born the second time like this, you need to have it happen.

No one has eternal life, no one shares in the kingdom of God, no person can truly be called a Christian until he turns to God and accepts this new life that Christ has made possible through His death for us on the cross and His resurrection.

This means asking God to forgive you and to help you follow Jesus Christ in a personal relationship. Only a person who has been born again, who has the Spirit of God in his life, has the power to live the Christian life as the Bible teaches it.

Is that so difficult? Yes, but not because it's hard to understand—what makes it difficult is that it involves a risk. What if you make that commitment and it doesn't work out? What if making that commitment should make you unattractive? What if all your friends think you're going off the deep end? What if your wife or husband or boyfriend or girlfriend doesn't understand? It *is* quite a risk to make a commitment to Jesus Christ. Being born again is not cheap.

But let me assure you, I have never seen a person whose commitment to Christ made him unattractive. Yes, there are unattractive Christians but it's not because God made them that way. Self-righteousness, defensiveness, pettiness —all of these bad qualities sometimes associated with Christianity are not from God. They are people's doings, distortions of the true Christian life-style we've been talking about.

The Bible says the Spirit of God will produce in us "love, joy, peace, patience, kindness, goodness, faithfulness, gentleness, self-control" (Galatians 5:22-23, NASB). These qualities can hardly be called unattractive.

So becoming a Christian *is* a risk. There is an element of the new and unknown, but I can assure you it is *never* a losing venture. Jesus Christ offers you a life that will be full and meaningful in a way you may never have dreamed possible.

So it's your decision. You can let the misconceptions of Christianity mislead you into not accepting Jesus Christ. Or you can step beyond the misconceptions and be born again into the reality of a new life in Jesus Christ and into God's family.

2
Secret
Christianity

Most people think of Christianity as a public religion. They think of long, wordy prayers and hour-long sermons. They remember confirmations or testimonies or other ways of publicly expressing faith in God. They think of a respected civic leader, whose Christianity leads him into charitable public service.

But there is a very different aspect of true Christianity, which is far more important than any of our pious, public performances. I call it "secret Christianity."

The Bible records in the sixth chapter of the book of Matthew a scene in which Jesus was talking to the religious leaders of Jerusalem, the Pharisees. He told them they were missing the whole point of why good deeds should be done.

"Take care!" He said. "Don't do your good deeds publicly, to be admired, for then you will lose the reward from your Father in heaven" (Matthew 6:1, LB).

Jesus was concerned because the Pharisees

only understood *public religion*. They were interested in impressing people. They wanted to look good. Jesus was saying that they were missing the boat—they weren't impressing God!

Usually a brand new Christian is a beautiful sight, but sometimes one particular problem sadly and needlessly plagues him. This problem could be called a "spiritual inferiority complex." The new Christian often enters a whole new world of customs that he is unfamiliar with. He can begin to feel second-rate because he doesn't know how to pray eloquently in public, or because he doesn't feel comfortable giving a two-minute sermonette on what Christ means to him.

The whole area of Bible knowledge looms before him, and he may see people around him who seem to know the whole thing by heart. Caught in this type of situation, he begins to feel like a second-class Christian.

God Sees Your Heart

But what does the Bible say? "God sees not as man sees, for man looks at the outward appearance, but the Lord looks at the heart" (1 Samuel 16:7, NASB).

Men are always caught up in judging people by outward appearances, but God can zero right in and see our hearts. He's the only One who knows what's really going on in your life. And you must remember that He's the only One whose opinion ultimately matters. He is the one and only Person who needs to know about the things you do for Him and for other people.

In New Testament times, a Jewish religious leader carried a little silver trumpet, and whenever he was going to do a good deed—perhaps give some bread to a beggar or assist a needy widow—he would blow his trumpet until a small crowd gathered around and then he would very dramatically do his deed of kindness.

That's what Jesus was talking about when He said, "When you give a gift to a beggar, don't shout it about as the hypocrites do—blowing trumpets in the synagogues and streets to call attention to their acts of charity! I tell you in all earnestness, they have received all the reward they will ever get" (Matthew 6:2, LB).

Jesus is saying, "Watch out for that type of thing. If you're into doing good deeds just for the publicity, your reward will be the scattered applause of the crowds that gather, that's all."

He says instead, "When you do a kindness to someone, do it secretly—don't tell your left hand what your right hand is doing. And your Father who knows all secrets will reward you" (Matthew 6:3-4, LB).

Don't make a big deal of your charity. Some famous personalities spend a lot of money and time promoting the charities they support. It may make them feel better to be known as charitable people. But God says, "It's enough to do the deed. You don't need a pat on the back from the public. In fact, you don't even need a pat on the back from *yourself*."

The most beautiful acts of mercy are private. There's a man who was drawn to the church where I pastor through a secret act of mercy by a family in our church.

"My father died very suddenly," he told me, "and a couple from your church left everything, took days off work, and hired a baby-sitter and flew out to Kansas City from Chicago to be with me." After spending several days with this person, the couple flew back and resumed their normal activities and no one else ever knew.

No one in our church will ever know who that couple is, but it doesn't matter. God knows. That's secret Christianity. The God who sees in secret will richly reward the family who rushed to help a man in need.

Another woman I know recently took two or three days off from work just to spend some time alone with her son. Her only desire was to convince her child that he was special. That's secret Christianity. No one knew about it but the three of us. But the God who sees in secret will be the God who rewards her.

Sometimes secret Christianity is hardly a matter of choice. I once had a two-day speaking engagement in Lincoln, Nebraska. I was just getting ready to board the plane for my return flight when a young mother came up to me and said, "I have an 11-month-old baby that I'd like you to hold on your lap to Chicago. When you get there, my mother—the baby's grandmother—will meet you and take the baby."

This was before my wife and I had our daughter, so I protested, "I don't know anything about babies!" But the woman assured me, "Oh the baby will be fine. She sleeps all the time." So I gave in. I took the baby and got on the plane.

No sooner had we gotten off the ground than the baby started to cry. She cried like you have never heard a baby cry in your life.

I was helpless. People in the seats around me

were getting annoyed but I couldn't make that little girl stop crying. Finally a woman came to my rescue and sat in the seat behind me and rocked the baby to sleep. What an angel of mercy!

Then as we were landing, the crying started all over again. And to top it all off, when I got off the plane, I couldn't find the grandmother. It took almost thirty minutes to make the contact. But the baby was finally transferred and my job was over. Perhaps I've spoiled this good deed by making it public, but really it's not your applause I'm seeking—just a little sympathy!

Now, let's get back on the track. Some Christians perform menial tasks without which the Body of Christ couldn't operate, but because they're not preachers or soloists or other "upfront" performers, they feel they're second-class Christians. They're not.

Whatever you do, if you do it in a spirit of love, for the cause of Christ, the God who sees in secret will reward in secret and He will richly bless your life. So keep on practicing secret Christianity, you first-class Christians! It's beautiful!

Jesus also had some things to say to the Pharisees about public and private prayer. He said, "When you pray, don't be like the hypocrites who pretend piety by praying publicly on street corners and in the synagogues where everyone can see them. Truly, that is all the reward they will ever get. But when you pray, go away by yourself, all alone, and shut the door behind you and pray to your Father secretly, and your Father, who knows your secrets, will reward you" (Matthew 6:5-6, LB).

So what is Jesus saying? The real first-class

prayer is not the eloquent public prayer, but the secret, private prayer—which doesn't have to be eloquent at all. This passage contains some specific instructions about prayer.

Go to a Private Place

Don't let anyone see you. Pray *privately*. Why? Because then there will be no confusion of motive. If you go to a private place, no one is going to peek in and admire you for being on your knees.

Also, when you go to a private place to be with God, you're demonstrating profound truth. You're telling God that you're willing to go out of your way to spend time alone with Him. It means you care enough about your secret relationship with God to make time for it.

Pray Directly to God the Father

Do business with God Himself, through Jesus Christ who has opened the door for us into God's presence. No Christian has a "hotter line" to God the Father than any other obedient Christian. Someone has said, "The ground is level at the foot of the Cross." Keep that in mind as you pray directly to the Father.

Forget "Religious Jargon"

Don't try to fill your prayers with just the right phraseology and the right words. Jesus said, "Do not use meaningless repetition, as the Gentiles do, for they suppose that they will be answered for their many words . . . for your Father knows what you need, before you ask Him" (Matthew 6:7-8, NASB).

Your prayers should be simple. Just talk with

God, friend to Friend, child to Father. Go away in secret, pray in secret, pray directly to God in your own words—and the God who sees in secret will reward you.

Fasting

Finally, Jesus talked about fasting. It was customary in His time to fast as a Jewish tradition. And the Pharisees were great ones at letting everyone know they were doing without food. They would allow themselves to look positively pitiful in order to advertise their fasting to the community.

Jesus' reaction to this was, of course, not complimentary to the Pharisees. He said, "When you fast, declining your food for a spiritual purpose, don't do it publicly, as the hypocrites do . . . so people will feel sorry for them. Truly, that is the only reward they will ever get. But when you fast, put on festive clothing, so that no one will suspect you are hungry, except your Father who knows every secret. And He will reward you" (Matthew 6:16-18, LB).

Today people fast for many reasons. Often it is done to symbolize a struggle for Christian growth. If you're fasting, or in *any* other way, trying to say to God, "I mean business," don't broadcast it. You can tell a close friend, but don't spread it around. That's second-class Christianity. Many people make drastic changes in their life-styles because they believe God wants them to. But no one should advertise these types of things. Don't tell the world what a sacrifice you're making.

Keep your personal sacrifices between God and yourself. He knows all about them. He knows how much you want to do His will. And as you grow, the God who sees you struggling in secret will reward you.

How exactly will God reward you? No one can tell you in a flat formula. He has rewarded me in different ways at different times. Sometimes it's been a passage of Scripture that came to life just when I needed it. Sometimes it's been just a sense of peace and security in the middle of a trying day or a hectic week.

God has the power to make beautiful things happen in your life. And there's really no end to the ways He might reward you for your secret acts of devotion and mercy.

It's also important to remember that we don't get all of our rewards here in this life. It is a consistent principle throughout the Bible that our rewards in heaven will correspond to our degree of mercy and kindness and devotion here on earth in our day-to-day lives.

Believe me, the God of the universe sees your secret acts of mercy and kindness. He knows. And you can be sure that He'll reward you. What a beautiful concept this is!

So don't worry about your eloquence. Don't let it bother you if you're aren't yet a Bible scholar. Don't feel second-class because you can't deliver prayers in the grand public tradition.

It's God we need to please. We need to pray to Him alone. And His are the only rewards worth having anyway.

3
Whom Not
To Listen To

Have you ever noticed that great people stand apart from the crowd?

If you study the history of art, you find that the artists who created works that outlast time, all seemed to have a spirit of individuality about themselves. They weren't affected very much by those around them, especially people who would have held them back.

Often they caught a lot of flak from their peers. They had to go broke and endure bad critical reviews and other hardships for the sake of creating what they felt was Art. Many of them died before their work was recognized or appreciated.

The same kind of pattern holds true in the history of God's people. The prophets of the Old Testament were men who stood apart from the nation of Israel and cried, "God says what you're doing is wrong!" They could have taken the comfortable way, the less dangerous way, but their consciences wouldn't let them. They were often beaten or stoned for their efforts.

Jesus, our foremost model of spiritual individuality, chose to speak out against the whole Jewish religious establishment of His day. And in the centuries between His time and ours, there have been many great leaders of the Christian church. Most of them were brave individuals who paid dearly for their allegiance to God's truth.

Christians in the Roman world often endured persecution because they wouldn't follow the crowd, but chose to follow Christ.

Martin Luther dared to step outside of the religious traditions of his day in order to make spiritual contributions that still affect our world.

The Pilgrims who migrated to America came here to exercise their spiritual individuality. They could have stayed in comfortable old England, but they stepped into the wild unknown to do what they felt God wanted them to do.

You and I face the same choices in our lives. We may not be Pilgrims or Martin Luthers, but we still must decide for ourselves whether we're going to follow the crowd or think and act for ourselves, according to what we sense God is telling us.

Jesus said, "What good is it for one blind man to lead another? He will fall into a ditch and pull the other down with him" (Luke 6:39, LB).

What He's saying is that we'd better be careful whom we listen to in this world, because not everybody knows where he's going. We don't need a leader who's going to pull us into a ditch after him.

Jesus continued, "Everyone, after he has been fully trained, will be like his teacher" (Luke 6:40, NASB). If this is true, we'd better choose our teachers pretty carefully.

As I read over these words of Jesus, I remember how impressionable I've been, how I used to read and listen to everything recommended to me by the teachers I respected. Some of it I regret, and some of it I don't. The point is, *I was drawn toward becoming like my leaders.*

It's a sad truth in our society that we've been programmed to think that everyone who publishes a book or gets his name on an album cover knows what truth is all about. Young people are often asked to assume that adults have the answers. Adults often feel that anyone with a Ph.D. or some other symbol of expertise has an inside track on truth.

In our society we seldom learn to put much stock in what *we ourselves* think life is all about.

As I look back on my short life, perhaps the three most important decisions I had to make were:

1. *Who would be my master?*
2. *Whom would I marry?* and
3. *What would be my career?*

Who Will Be My Master?

When I was 15, my friends found out that I was interested in Christianity. They really gave me a hard time.

"Bill, you're freaking out!" they said. "Don't do that! Jesus is for strange people, people who need a crutch! You don't need God!"

And for a period of time, I listened to my friends. I let them tell me what was true and what wasn't. I was very impressionable at that stage of my life. This went on for years before I began to realize, after some hard times, that maybe *I* ought to have a say in the matter.

I was running my life by parliamentary procedure, taking votes among my friends. Suddenly it dawned on me: *This is my only life.* Why should someone else or some group of friends run *my* life?

So I made a decision. I decided that I should be man enough to investigate Christianity if I felt that it might have some answers for me. So I did. In fact, I went so far as to ask Jesus Christ into my life, even though it wasn't a popular thing to do. I refused, finally, to let my peers run my life.

Now, eight or nine years later, I look around at the people who told me not to investigate Christianity, and what do I find? The head spokesman for that little group of friends is dead. He committed suicide a few years ago. He couldn't handle life any longer.

A couple of the other leading members of my peer group have gone through divorces, and now their children are growing up in broken homes. A couple more are so strung out on pills and other escapes that they're no good to anybody.

So I sit today and think to myself, *Wow. I let those guys run my life for years . . . and what did they know?*

The most important decision in your life is this: *Who will be your master?* Whom are you going to follow? Will it be the trends and fads of the world around you? Jesus says that's just like letting a blind man lead you around. You'll both wind up in the ditch.

Maybe you'll choose some poet or philosopher. I was counseling once with a woman and asked her, "What do you think about the life hereafter?"

"I believe my candle goes out," she said. "Then there's nothingness forever."

"That's very interesting," I told her. "Where do you get this belief?"

"I heard someone say it one time," she replied.

This woman was staking her whole future after death on something she'd heard someone say, *and she didn't even remember who said it!*

"You know, you're going to be dead a lot longer than you're going to be alive here on earth," I told her. "Don't you think you ought to check this person out? Maybe he didn't mean it. Maybe he's changed his mind since then. It wouldn't be the first time a philosopher changed his mind."

At a point in Jesus' ministry when many people had decided not to follow Him, He asked His disciples if they too were going to leave Him.

"Simon Peter replied, 'Master, to whom shall we go? You alone have the words that give eternal life' " (John 6:68, LB).

I want to challenge you to compare the wisdom of your peer group or your pet philosopher with the wisdom of Jesus Christ as recorded in the Bible. *Then* decide who is worthy to be your master.

Whom Will I Marry?

After I decided to allow Jesus Christ to be my master, I had another very important decision to make. Whom would I choose for a wife? As simple as that is for some people, it was a pretty complicated decision for me.

You see, I grew up in a unique subculture. According to that culture, "If you weren't Dutch, you weren't much!" And if you weren't thoroughbred

Dutch, you were a cut under the acceptable standard.

So when it came time for us "bionic race" Dutchmen to choose wives, we were expected to follow an unwritten rule that said we would marry Dutch girls. That way we wouldn't "spoil the blood."

Well, it just so happened that I wasn't too impressed with Dutch girls. And there was this one young Englishwoman that I thought was just right. So I took her home and said, "Mom and Dad, I think this is the one." And it turned out that they really liked her, but not as much (at first) as they would have *liked* to like her.

To make a long story short, I had to decide whether to follow my heart or my subculture. I chose my heart. But it wasn't just a matter of "following my feelings"—of doing what *I* thought *I* wanted to do. Lynne was godly, confident, gentle, spiritual, and comfortable to be with. I knew she could help me a great deal in every area of my life. I really had the assurance that she was the girl God had for me.

Perhaps your decision in this area is of a different nature than mine. Perhaps you've found someone you love, but he or she doesn't fit the acceptable standard of your culture in some other way.

Our society puts a high priority on material success. Girls are sometimes made to feel that the best choice for a husband is always the one with the best chances of being "successful" in the future. Guys in our culture are subconsciously encouraged to marry the girl with the most outward beauty. If you fall in love with someone who doesn't fit those criteria, you have a difficult decision to make.

To reject the acceptable standards of your culture may be one of the toughest decisions you ever make. But the pain you suffer will be nothing compared to the peace you get from *knowing* that you've made the right choice. In a society where a solid, happy marriage is a rare thing, it's valuable to know that God offers to help us choose our mates.

What Will Be My Career?

Once I had decided who was going to be my master, once I had chosen a wife, then one more big choice confronted me—what was I going to do with my life?

Again I had to work against a predetermined plan. My father owns a successful wholesale produce company. When I was born, my parents took one look at me and said, "He's going to be a produce man." They could tell by my hands, I guess. They must have thought they looked like cucumber-picking hands.

At 17, I was buying produce on the Chicago market and driving one of our company's trucks. I enrolled in college as a business major. My whole life was laid out for me.

But it wasn't enough. As my commitment to Christ matured, I realized that in heaven God wasn't going to ask me how many cases of lettuce I had sold.

God *does call* many people to the business work. Christian men and women are needed in *every* walk of life. However, I knew God was calling *me* to a different kind of work and I had to respond.

So I made my choice—from the heart and regardless of pressures to do otherwise. I've never
once regretted it.

As I look back, I can see that my life was affected by whom I listened to, especially God Himself. But it was also greatly affected by my choos-
ing *not* to listen to certain people. God gives every
genuine Christian a sense of direction in
decision-making.

Watch For Authenticity

First, any person whom you let influence your life
should be an *authentic* person. Jesus had plenty to
say about people who came along with impressive
words, but have empty hearts. For example, "Beware of false teachers who come disguised as
harmless sheep, but are wolves and will tear you
apart. You can detect them by the way they act,
just as you can identify a tree by its fruit"
(Matthew 7:15-16, LB.).

It's not what people *say* that is the final crite-
rion here; *it's how they live out what they say*. God
has given us all the ability to sense when someone
is genuine. And I believe He also helps us know
when that genuineness is lacking. Teachers,
peers, co-workers—they all have "words of wisdom" to offer us. But if we don't see a life-style to
back up those words and we don't sense a sincere
concern for us as individuals, then those people
are nothing more than blind guides—and we are
nothing more than sightless followers.

I can remember thinking about my high school
friends, *You're telling me what I need and don't
need—but your own lives are falling apart. Why
should I listen to you?*

Watch For "Ceiling-Builders"

Secondly, any person who is truly going to help you should give you complete freedom to reach your highest spiritual potential. In other words, if someone tries to put a ceiling on your spiritual growth, watch out. A balloon filled with helium will quietly float out of sight when it's let go into the sky, but how far will it go upward in your living room?

The same kind of limitation can be put on your growth as a Christian if you are placed in certain negative situations. You may find yourself with a group of friends or in a church that sets low spiritual standards. The result will be mediocrity and a lukewarm Christian life.

Sometimes members of your own family may unintentionally try to put a ceiling on your spiritual growth with comments such as, "Don't go off the deep end," or "You're taking your commitment to Christ too seriously." These people aren't necessarily trying to mess you up, they simply don't understand the meaning of Christian commitment.

Jesus said, "If anyone comes to Me, and does not hate his own father and mother and wife and children and brothers and sisters, yes, and even his own life, he cannot be My disciple" (Luke 14:26, NASB).

What Jesus is talking about here is not literal hate, but the ability to be free of all influences that would hold you back from your full spiritual potential in Him. When it's all said and done, what's important in your life is that you grow closer to God. That means you should keep a healthy skepticism for all individuals, groups, or counselors who attempt to limit your growth as a Christian.

Life is full of cheap bumper-sticker philosophies and well-meaning advisers. There are also some not so well-meaning hucksters out there, the "wolves" that Jesus talked about, who preach a good line, but who are really out to exploit you.

You have only one life to lead here on earth. There are no reruns or extra innings. Every day is important. Each decision you make counts. The Bible says that when you become a Christian, God has a mission for you—you'd better find out what it is, then give it all you've got.

There will come a point in time when you will stand alone before God. He's not going to ask you what your friends or your parents or your pastor thought. He's going to say something like this:

"My son, (My daughter) you heard My soft prompting. You read My Bible. Did you respond authentically as an individual or did others run your life?"

And I hope at that point you'll be able to answer something like this:

"There was a world full of great pretenders, Lord, but I know that only You had the wisdom to direct my life. You showed me that money, popularity, and power weren't the right goals for me.

"My path was focused on You, Lord. And it was full and exciting like no other life could have been. It was solid and special in a way none of the temporary exits could ever be."

To whom will you listen? Your life can go as high with Jesus Christ as you're willing to let it go. There's no limit with Him. The real question is whether you'll close your ears to the garbled

messages of the blind guides and really tune in to
Jesus.

4
God Thinks
I'm Special

What does God think about you?

In view of your past, your personality, your hang ups—what do you think God's opinion of you really is? Do you sometimes wonder if He even sees you in the vast sea of human personalities He has created?

Philosophers have wrestled with this question for centuries, taking varying views on the ultimate nature of God's feelings toward humanity. Many of us try to understand how God feels about us an individuals, but seldom do we succeed. Vast numbers of other people are afraid to even think about it.

The only way to come to grips with God's opinion of people is to look in the Bible. A very familiar verse, John 3:16, reads, "For God so loved the world (the people in it), that He gave His only begotten Son, that whoever believes in Him should not perish, but have eternal life" (NASB).

Many people are familiar with this verse, but what does it *mean?* How should it affect our lives?

How do we begin to understand that God loves us as individuals?

The President Loves Me!

Let's imagine that some Sunday morning I've just finished a message at our church and all the membership (including me) is filing out of the building. We look across the street and there's a flag-draped platform that's been erected in the middle of the parking lot. Six or eight black limousines are parked nearby and a large crowd is gathering.

So all of us run over to see what's going on, and there's a very familiar face up there! The President of the United States is standing on the platform getting ready to make a speech! By the time he begins to speak, an enormous crowd has filled the whole parking lot.

"You're probably wondering," the President begins, "why I'm here today—why I wanted all of you to be here too. It's for one person's sake. One person. And if he's in the audience, I'd like to ask him to step forward—*Bill Hybels.*"

That would really be something, wouldn't it? So here I go. I run up onto the platform and stand beside the President. He's smiling at me. I'm smiling back. *What next?* I'm wondering.

"Do you see this fella right here?" he asks the audience. "I've come all the way from Washington to tell you I think a lot of this guy. In fact, I'm compelled to tell you, *I love Bill Hybels.*

"I'd give up my office for him if I had to," says the President. All the people are applauding and cheering by now. My wife is crying. They've *never* seen anything like this.

"When it comes right down to it," concludes the Chief Executive, "if someone asked me to exchange my very life for this man's, I would do it."

Now let's say that really happened—that little scene I've just described. *You* know how I'd feel when I stepped down from that platform—I'd be walking around saying, "It's *me—the guy the President loves!* I'm the guy he said he'd give up the White House for, the guy he'd die for!"

If I had a flat tire on the way home, you think I'd get bummed out? No way. If I made some mistakes later in the week, you think I'd condemn myself? How could I? *The President loves me!* I'd think to myself. I would know I was special in the eyes of someone extremely important—perhaps the most influential man on this planet. Wouldn't it be great to be loved by someone like that?

You are.

You are loved by Someone a whole lot more famous than the President will ever be. This Person's love is infinitely stronger than the President's imaginary love for me—and best of all, it isn't imaginary. It's real. And it's something you and I don't often appreciate.

"For God so loved the world, that He sent His only begotten Son . . ." In other words, God said, "I love all persons on earth so much that I'll make the ultimate sacrifice for them." That's how much God loves us.

Jesus said, "What is the price of five sparrows? A couple of pennies? Not much more than that. Yet God does not forget a single one of them. And He knows the number of hairs on your head! Never fear, you are far more valuable to Him than a whole flock of sparrows" (Luke 12:6-7, LB).

In God's eyes, each of us is special and precious. That fact ought to change our lives. Do you know that when you walk around feeling sorry for yourself, thinking that you're not a very special person, you're telling God that His great love doesn't impress you?

When a person comes to my office and tells me, "I'm having a problem liking myself—I'm so worthless," I usually say something like this:

"You must be worth *something,* God wouldn't allow His own Son Jesus to die for you if you were just a worthless individual. God doesn't make a practice of spilling innocent blood for no reason."

If you can capture just a little glimmer of what it means to be loved by Someone as important and powerful as God, it can turn your whole life around.

Did you know there's going to come a time when you can experience a demonstration of love much like the one I imagined with the President? Jesus said, "If anyone publicly acknowledges Me as his Friend, I will openly acknowledge him as My friend before My Father in heaven" (Matthew 10:32, LB).

This means that there is going to come a time when Jesus Christ will take each of His followers and stand before everyone who ever lived and say to God the Father, "Here he is, My Father, a very special friend. I love this person. I died for this person and he accepted that gift and we're friends. I present him to You faultless and blameless and pure" (Jude v. 24).

Then the grandstands will break out in a thunderous roar of approval. It's going to be great.

I hope I can learn to keep that future event in

mind as I live every day as a child of God. I wish all of God's children could. What changes we'd see in people's lives!

Mission: Unbelievable

Now let's imagine that a couple of weeks after my adventure with the President, I get a phone call one morning from the Pentagon. It's one of the Chiefs of Staff calling.

"Is this Bill Hybels?" he asks gruffly.

"Yes, sir."

"We've been watching you for the last three or four years," he says, "and we have a special mission for you. It's something only you can accomplish. You're just right for it. You're just the right height, just the right weight, you have just the right intellect—which means it requires no brains at all! It's a vital mission, Bill; it's got to be done."

"Well—"

"Let me add," the Chief says solemnly, "if you take this mission you'll have a great impact for good on some people's lives, but if you turn it down, their lives may be lost. They'll suffer for your lack of courage."

"Wow. I—"

"But I've got to warn you," he says, "there will be times when you'll think you were out of your mind to accept this mission. It'll be tough sometimes. The pay is lousy and the hours are terrible.

"People will take advantage of you, Bill. Every bit of your intellect, your emotional strength, and your spiritual strength will be challenged. It will be the hardest job you ever tackled. But it will also be the most exciting. There'll be daring rescues, last-minute escapes, awesome opposition—"

"*(Gulp)* Well, I don't know—"

"But," the Chief interrupts, "it will also be very fulfilling. When you're finished, you'll look back and say, 'Boy, am I glad I wasn't afraid to take on this challenge. I'm glad I didn't just sit in front of my TV while the world went to hell.'"

"And finally, Bill," says the Chief, "there are rewards. We'll pin so many medals on your chest that you'll be top-heavy. We'll not forget what you've done for us. Well, Bill, are you up for it? Are you still there?"

"Oh, I'm still here all right," I tell him. "And I know what my answer is."

The parallel here should be obvious. God the Father has a special mission for each one of us. He has a plan for us that takes into consideration our unique talents and gifts. The Bible says, "We are His workmanship, created in Christ Jesus for good works, which God prepared beforehand, that we should walk in them" (Ephesians 2:10, NASB).

But God doesn't just offer His children this plan as a casual take-it-or-leave-it affair. He expects us to accept our missions. He means business. The Apostle Paul puts it this way: "I plead with you to give your bodies to God. Let them be a living sacrifice, holy—the kind He can accept. When you think of what He has done for you, is this too much to ask?" (Romans 12:1, LB).

The world doesn't need any more pick-and-choose Christians, trying to choose for themselves the areas where they will and will not obey God. If you say "No" to a general in the Pentagon, that may or may not be too serious. But if you're a born-again child of God and you say "No" to Him, you're making a big mistake. You are making a mockery of Christ's death for you *and* cutting yourself off from a beautiful lifelong adventure.

You'll never know what the vital Christian life is all about until you take God up on His offer of a special mission for your life. That's what Jesus meant when He said, "If anyone wishes to come after Me, let him deny himself, and take up his cross daily, and follow Me. For whoever wishes to save his life shall lose it, but whoever loses his life for My sake, he is the one who will save it" (Luke 9:23-24, NASB).

God is not playing games. He's looking for Christians who will turn over their lives to Him so that He can use them to change the direction of the great drama of history. Jesus said, "All of us must quickly carry out the tasks assigned to us by the One who sent Me, for there is little time left before the night falls and all work comes to an end" (John 9:4, LB).

Jesus Christ has important missions for each of us. The question is, will we accept our missions as true followers of Jesus? Or will we turn them down and go back to rot in front of our TVs?

AT&T'S New Device

Let's say I've already been through this great period in my life, with a personal commendation from the President and now this new mission from the Pentagon. Now I get a phone call from a representative of AT&T.

"I hear the President thinks you're pretty special, Bill," he says.

"Yeah, well, shucks—"

"I also hear that you've signed up to be a part of

this mission thing, one of these special projects from the Pentagon."

"Yep. I think it's a great opportunity," I tell him.

"Well, then you're entitled to the newest device from Bell laboratories," he replies.

"Really? Can you show me one?"

"I can't. It's invisible."

"Well, what does it do?" I ask. I'm pretty curious by this time.

"It does a lot of things," the AT&T rep says. "First of all, it goes with you wherever you go. It hovers right around the area of your heart. It doesn't freeze when it's cold. It doesn't melt when it's hot. It'll stay with you no matter what you're doing."

"This all sounds fine," I tell him, "but what are the real advantages of having this device?"

"Wait till you hear!" he says. "To begin with, whenever you're about to make a wrong decision, this device sort of beeps and says, '*Ah, ah—be careful.*' Then you can reconsider and have another chance to make the right decision.

"Then it does some other things too. It has the ability to make you feel like you're never alone. When you feel lonely, it has a way of sending out waves to your mind and you'll realize, *Hey, I may not have any other people around, but my little device is right here with me.*

"That would be nice sometimes," I have to agree with him.

"Yes, it can comfort you," he says, "but that's not all."

"There's more?"

"Yes. It has a way of steering you down the path

that will be the best possible path for your life. And it helps you in your comprehension of your mission—and lots, lots more. I'm sure you'd like one, wouldn't you?"

"Yeah," I say. "Sure I would."

"Well, it just so happens that you qualify to get one *free.* You see, it's free to all people who have received the President's personal commendation and who have accepted their special missions from the Pentagon. We'll send it to you right away."

By this time, I'm sure that most readers have caught the parallel here, too. The Holy Spirit is God's special mobile communications Center who takes up residence in every Christian. But the Holy Spirit is infinitely more impressive than any AT&T James Bond plaything on the market.

For example, a device from the technocrats might malfunction after a while; but not the Holy Spirit. With Him there is not the remotest chance of failure.

Like the AT&T device I described, the Holy Spirit goes with us everywhere, gives us comfort and direction, and helps us when our backs are against the wall.

But there the similarity ends and the uniqueness of the Holy Spirit begins.

The greatest characteristic of this Holy Spirit who is available to all Christians is that He is a *Person.* He is not a device. He is an equal Member of the Trinity. He is God. But how does He get into God's plan?

Shortly before His crucifixion, Jesus told His disciples, "I tell you the truth: It is for your good that I am going away. Unless I go away, the

Counselor will not come to you; but if I go, I will send Him to you" (John 16:7, NIV).

Jesus ascended into heaven 40 days after His resurrection. That's what He meant by "going away." He then sent the Holy Spirit, as promised, to His followers on the day of Pentecost. He sent "the Counselor" to them. Why does He say this is "for your good"?

Jesus, even though He could perform miracles, did not change the fact that He was *geographically limited* in His human body. He could not be in more than one place at the same time. But after He went back to heaven, He sent the Holy Spirit who (don't ask me how) *can be with all of God's children at the same time no matter where they are or what they're doing.*

And what does Jesus say the Holy Spirit will do for us?

"He will guide you into all truth" (John 16:13, NIV).

"He will tell you what is yet to come" (v. 13).

So Jesus says the Holy Spirit will lead us into all truth, He'll tell us what we need to know about the future, and He'll help us understand God's word and God's creation.

In the language of Madison Avenue, *that's quite a package.*

But remember, the Holy Spirit is for Christians only. And the real power of the Holy Spirit is only released as Christians commit themselves completely to the special "mission" that God assigns to them.

God has work for you to do. It's not drudgery. It's tough, challenging, meaningful work. It's an assignment for which He has given you unique abilities so you can carry it out.

I may dream of the President coming to see me, but God has already traveled all the way from heaven to our little messed-up planet to see us, to die for us.

I may dream of a "special mission." But God has one for me that's more important than any espionage assignment the Pentagon could come up with.

I may dream of a special "device" to help me in my "mission," but God has given me a Person to perform functions for me that no electronic gadget will ever be able to perform.

When I look at these facts, I can begin to see how God feels about me. God thinks I'm pretty important. He wouldn't do all that He's done and all that He's still doing if He didn't think highly of me. God knows what my faults are. But I'm special to Him *just because He created me.*

God thinks I'm special.

And He thinks you're special, too. If you don't believe it, it's not because He hasn't tried to tell you.

5
God Has
Feelings Too

I've had the opportunity to travel in many countries of the world, and I've seen lots of interesting sights. But there's one picture that always sticks sadly in my memory. I've seen it more than once.

It's a picture of some person, usually someone poor and needy, pouring out his soul to an idol. If you ever see a human being get down on his knees and release his innermost feelings to a cold chunk of stone, you'll never forget it.

It makes me hurt inside. I feel like crying, "My friend, how can you do it? You're a feeling, thinking, human being and you're praying to a cold, lifeless nonentity! Wake up!"

But you don't have to travel to some far land to see people praying to a cold, lifeless deity. Many *Christians* have a cool and detached concept of the God of the Bible. They pray to God as if He's as impersonal and removed as a piece of stone. Lots of people haven't yet learned that our God is a *feeling* God. We have feelings and we're made in His image. God has feelings too.

The Lord of the universe understands my feelings and your feelings. Jesus Christ can identify with our hurts and joys. He became a human. He knows how it feels.

This means a lot to me, because when I've got a hurt and I run to Jesus Christ with it, I know that He cares about my situation. He's concerned and sensitive. He knows how I feel because He's been through the human struggle, emotions and all.

Knowing that God has feelings is related to the heart of Christianity. What is Christianity, anyway? We've said it isn't just a religion. It isn't a set of rituals. It's not a list of restrictions or resolutions. *Christianity is a relationship*—a living relationship with God.

Now a relationship between two persons means there must be feelings going back and forth. It's pretty difficult to have a relationship with a person who's in a coma—it's all one-sided. It's hard to have a relationship with any person who for some reason doesn't respond emotionally. In fact, it's impossible. If you don't believe it, try it sometime.

So if we're going to have a meaningful relationship with God, *there must be feelings going back and forth*. We need to presuppose and then *experience* that our relationship with God is one of mutual emotion, with feelings passing both ways. Our feelings go to Him and His feelings come to us.

Perhaps you haven't thought about God as an emotional Being, but the Bible clearly shows that He is. The Old Testament tells how God created man to be with Him, close to Him. But what happened? Man chose his own path of disobedience.

Did God give up on the human race? No. He determined to win people back. He said, in effect, "I'm going to love you back to Myself. I'll overwhelm you with love and then maybe you'll open up your lives to Me and we can resume a close friendship with each other."

But still people refused God's love. They turned their backs on Him, as they do yet today. This caused so much emotional upheaval in God's heart that He said through the prophet Hosea, "My heart cries out within Me; how I long to help you!" (Hosea 11:8, LB)

Here is the God of the universe passionately crying out to His people! This is not some ordinary "I-love-you-will-you-love-me?" relationship. This is almighty God saying, "Come to Me. Please. Please!" His emotions are *real*.

So that we can better understand that God has feelings, let's examine four of God's primary emotions.

Love

The first is His predominant emotion, and I'm sure you know what it is. God's deepest feeling for all of His people and for the world is *love*. The Bible says that "Love is the essence and nature of God" (1 John 4:8). Love is God's nature. It's His deepest feeling and the primary motive for everything He does.

Some people think that God's primary emotion is hatred. They cower through life, afraid of making errors or causing waves. God for them is no more than some threatening cosmic policeman.

But look at how God Himself expresses His feelings:

"When Israel [the nation] was a child I loved him as a son and brought him out of Egypt. . . . I trained him from infancy; I taught him to walk, I held him in My arms. But he doesn't know or even care that it was I who raised him" (Hosea 11:1-3, LB).

God is saying here, "I really take care of My children. My overwhelming feeling for them is one of love. If they'd just receive My love, we could continue in a beautiful relationship."

Frustration

But you and I know that this doesn't usually happen. Often we don't receive the love that God offers. And so this introduces God's second primary emotion—*frustration*. Did you know that you can frustrate God? Did you know that you can put almighty God in a state of tension and exasperation? Yes, you can. Many people feel that God is immovable, that we couldn't do anything to upset Him or bring tension into His heart. But it happens.

"What shall I do with you?" God cries through Hosea the prophet. "For your love vanishes like morning clouds, and disappears like dew. . . . I don't want your sacrifices—I want your love, I don't want your offerings—I want you to know Me!" (Hosea 6:4-6, LB)

That's God talking to His people a few centuries before Christ. And He feels that same way today. When people turn their backs and say "So what!" to His love, it frustrates God. *"What am I going to do with you?"* He asks.

Even after a person has asked Christ to enter his life, he can still frustrate God. There have been opportunities that I've shied away from, out of fear, and I know God was frustrated. He wanted me to step out and trust Him, but I was afraid. Sometimes I sense Him asking me, "What am I going to do with you, Bill?"

If you have been turning off God's love or if you haven't been listening to the promptings He's been bringing into your life, He's probably saying to you, "What should I do with you? Do I punish you or love you more?"

Don't ever think that God is so far above us that He can't be touched by emotion. I come from a pious background—a very theologically stern background where people seem to tell you, "Don't worry, little peon. Don't worry, you puny little person. God will have His way. You can't affect Him one way or the other." I used to think that was the humble way of looking at life.

But that's not how the Bible tells it. It *matters* to God what we do. And He doesn't force His will on us. After the crowds had turned against Him, Jesus cried out to the city of Jerusalem, "How often I have wanted to gather your children together as a hen gathers her chicks beneath her wings, but you wouldn't let Me" (Matthew 23:37, LB).

That's not a picture of a stoic God who has frozen all emotion into cool steel. He's hopelessly in love with you and me and He's committed to restoring communion with us. So when any of us slams the door in His face, God is frustrated.

"What am I going to do with you?" He asks.

Anger

The third primary emotion of God is *anger*. I don't

usually dwell on this one too much, because people seem to sense it enough as it is. Those who are weighted down with guilt often think of God's personality as a perennially brooding thundercloud. God as revealed to us in Jesus Christ is *not primarily* an angry God, but He does have occasion to let anger well up inside of Him under certain circumstances.

Here's a description of how His anger builds up, taken again from the book of Hosea:

"I alone am God, your Lord, and have been ever since I brought you out of Egypt. You have no God but Me, for there is no other Saviour. I took care of you in the wilderness, in that dry and thirsty land. But when you had eaten and were satisfied, then you became proud and forgot Me" (Hosea 13:4-6, LB).

These words ring with feeling. God is saying, "After I took care of you so lovingly, you got proud and forgot all about Me." So what is His reaction?

"I will come upon you like a lion, or a leopard lurking along the road. I will rip you to pieces like a bear whose cubs have been taken away, and like a lion I will devour you" (Hosea 13:7-8, LB).

Don't think that God is so overwhelmingly loving that you can just get away with anything. His patience has a limit. If you repeatedly forget about Him, don't deceive yourself; He doesn't take it lightly.

So then is God some supreme egotist who demands our admiration? Is He saying we'd better stay in line because He deserves our loyalty?

No. The reason that we can't take God lightly is found in Jesus Christ. Just as God went out of His way to protect Israel, He has made the supreme sacrifice for us in sending His Son to suffer and die for us. He says to us, in effect, "I gave My Son Jesus Christ to suffer and die for you on the cross. I submitted a part of Myself to torture for your benefit. Don't slap Me in the face by ignoring what Christ has done for you."

There's a lesson in the book of Exodus about ingratitude to God. The people of Israel were blessed by the Lord. He led them safely out of Egypt and provided their every need. God even sent them bread from heaven—manna—to eat when they were wandering in the desert.

What was their reaction? Grumbling, ingratitude, faithlessness. And they paid for their ingratitude.

So it is today. God is saying to us, "If I provide for your needs and you turn right around and forget Me and say you don't need Me, watch out! You're on thin ice!"

"If I bless you financially and you become selfish, watch it!"

"If I bless you with a healthy baby and you turn around and forget about the people whose babies aren't so healthy and you show no compassion, watch out!"

The truth is, a Christian owes his entire life to God. Without Christ, we really have nothing. Because He has died for us and makes a new life possible for us, we owe Him everything.

That's a sobering thought, but perhaps it's not bad to be sobered once in a while. We may need to lower our "flippancy level." You know what a flippant person can sound like—he comes on with one of two approaches. Either he doesn't take God seriously enough to give his life to Christ, or else he doesn't worry about how his life should be led after entering into a relationship with Jesus Christ.

If we do know Jesus Christ, it's not enough to glibly say, "Things are great. Sure I'm growing. No major hassles, no big problems, right?"

We need to be careful in our claims about the "greatness" of our lives in Christ. God expects the best we can offer Him. The Bible says it's only reasonable and logical to offer our bodies as a "living sacrifice"—that is, to do with as He wants. This makes sense when we consider the richness of life He offers us.

It makes sense that God would get angry when we forget Him or ignore Him through our lives. What can you do that will hurt God more than anything else? Just ignore Him.

You see, what He wants more than anything else is communion with you. He has paid a great price so that He could be close to you. So if you want to hurt God's feelings, just be proud and say, "Who needs Him?" Or maybe you'd never say it, but you may show it by the way you live.

May God help us never to forget Him and become proud. We need Him. We need to commune with God. We need to be obedient to Him and talk with Him and live for Him, instead of giving Him a reason to be angry with us.

Forgiveness

Perhaps it's necessary to remind ourselves again that anger is not God's predominant emotion. I hope you never feel that way. His predominant emotion is *love*. We can bring on frustration and we can bring on *anger*—but after anger, God will say something like this:

"Return to the Lord, your God, for you have been crushed by your sins. Bring your petition. Come to the Lord and say, O Lord, take away our sins; be gracious to us and receive us, and we will offer You the sacrifice of praise" (Hosea 14:1-2, LB).

God is saying, "Turn back to Me. Don't assume that My anger is unchangeable. Ask Me. Ask Me for forgiveness!"

This is God's fourth primary emotion—*forgiveness*. God tells His people in the book of Hosea that if they will turn to Him, He will "cure them of idolatry and faithlessness" and His love will "know no bounds." He tells them His mercies will "never fail."

When people turn to God and ask Him for forgiveness, He takes them in with open arms; He forgives them. Then, He says, His mercies will never fail them. What more could we ask?

Does God want us to stay near Him so that He can keep us from having fun and make life hard on us? No. You see, God made us. He made our minds and our taste buds and our nerves and our innermost souls and *He knows how to make us truly fulfilled and happy*. That's why He wants us to stay close to Him—so He can show us what life was meant to be in all its fullness.

If you learn to walk with God and sense His presence every day throughout the day, your life is going to be more positive and exciting than you ever dreamed it could be. The Bible says, "Draw near to God and He will draw near to you" (James 4:8, NASB). But how can you draw near to God if you feel He's some cold, impersonal, removed

Being hiding out in the clouds somewhere? How can you draw near to Him if you think he isn't moved by your personal dilemma?

I hope you can see this isn't the case. God has deep feelings, and when you need Him to be sensitive, He's sensitive. Do you need comfort? Jesus Christ says, "Come to me, all [of you] who are weary and heavy laden, and I will give you rest" (Matthew 11:28, NASB).

When you need God to be forgiving and gentle, He says, "Come to Me. My mercies will never fail you."

But if you get stubborn and you're closing doors in His face, and you're passing up opportunities that God is giving you, then God is just like a father who really cares for his children. He says, "Wake up! My anger is kindled because you're missing out! Your own sins are crushing you. Get back on the path where you belong."

I'm thankful that God deals with us in anger sometimes, because if He was always buddy-buddy like we sometimes want Him to be, we'd miss out on the beauty of being corrected. "What's the beauty of being corrected?" you may ask. It's *finding that God has brought you back to the best path for your life.*

So if you're drifting and you sense that God is telling you to get back on the path where you belong, then say to Him, "Thank You, Lord. Without Your voice, I'd be following every Tom, Dick, and Harry who tried to persuade me to do something in this life. Thank You for bringing me back to the right path."

God has feelings. He has deep feelings about us, His children. He wants our lives to be full, interesting, and exciting.

His overwhelming emotion is that of intense love for you and me. When we're disloyal to God, we frustrate Him. When we're habitually disobedient to Him, He becomes angry. Not only are we ripping Him off of the love and loyalty that we owe Him, but we're missing out on the fulfillment that He wants to give us.

However, if we take one step toward Him, if we ask God to forgive us, He'll throw His arms around us and say, "Welcome back! My mercy will know no bounds. Stay with Me and you'll see what I mean."

If you have felt far away from God because you've thought of Him as cold and impersonal, I challenge you to do what James suggests (4:8). Draw near to God and you'll find out what He's really like. He won't disappoint you.

6
What If I Fall?

A few years ago I had the opportunity to get a pilot's license. The company that our family owns has two planes: a large one and also a smaller "Volkswagen" style of airplane. That's the one I fly.

On the dashboard of this small plane is an interesting little instrument called a *stall warning indicator*. The stall warning indicator is there to help the pilot avoid big trouble. In a light plane, if you get below a certain speed, you'll fall right out of the sky. On this particular plane the stall speed is 55 miles an hour. If you get below 55, say your prayers.

If your airspeed drops to around 60 miles an hour, you begin to hear a buzzer—the stall warning indicator is doing its thing.

When that buzzer begins to squawk and the corresponding red light begins to flash, you know "you're close to losing control!" So if you're climbing a little too fast, put the nose down, gain some speed and thank God for that stall warning indicator. It's a built-in device to help you avoid tragedy.

In your life, when you make a decision to follow Christ, God's own Spirit, the Holy Spirit, comes into you. Your body becomes a container, a house. The Bible calls your body a *temple* for the Holy Spirit (see 1 Corinthians 6:19-20).

It's the Holy Spirit within you that acts as a stall warning indicator, warning you and helping you to avoid tragedy. The Holy Spirit tells you when you're moving away from God and into danger.

Of course, just as the Holy Spirit tells you when you're getting far away from God's will so He also tells you when you're *very close* to God. One evening a friend and I took off from Meigs Field in downtown Chicago. We flew along the lakefront, past the Standard Oil Building, the John Hancock Building, and the Sears Tower. The sun was going down, the moon was rising, and the air was still and clear.

My friend and I looked at each other—we knew we were sharing the same thoughts. We could feel the closeness of God. We could sense His presence there with us.

That's because the Holy Spirit inside of us was confirming the presence of God. All Christians can tell you about experiences like this—when the Holy Spirit lets them know that God is very near. The Bible says that Christians have *fellowship* with God. He's with us, and we can believe it and know it.

So the Holy Spirit tells us that God is close to us *and* He warns us when there's a tragedy about to happen, just like a stall warning indicator. When we begin to make an error, when we start to choose our way instead of God's way, the Holy Spirit gives us a little jolt and says, "Watch out! You're getting off God's path and that means bad consequences! Be careful!"

Everybody's Human

I'm so glad I have the Holy Spirit in my life because, believe it or not, pastors make mistakes just like everybody else. Sometimes people think pastors have an inside track on spirituality, but it's just not true.

I stumble. I fall. And I disappoint the Person I love most—Jesus Christ. And when I do, I'm reminded of the consequences coming, because the Holy Spirit inside me says, "Bill, you're doing it again. Stop! Stop before you really do damage to your relationship with Jesus!"

That's what is called *conviction*—the Holy Spirit convicting a person of making an error. And it happens to all of us. Everyone—no matter how spiritually mature he is, no matter how firm his commitment to Christ—stumbles and makes mistakes and disappoints God.

The greatest men in the Bible were human— they made mistakes. My favorite Bible character is David. He was so close to God that God said, "I have found David . . . a man after My heart, who will do all My will" (Acts 13:22, NASB).

David was special in God's eyes, so you might get the idea that he was perfect. But he wasn't. You may already know the story. David committed adultery with Bathsheba and then committed murder to cover up the sin. He wasn't perfect. He was human just like the rest of us.

Peter was one of the disciples who was closest to

Jesus. He eventually became the leader of the church of Jerusalem. But he denied Christ three times. He said, "I don't know Him!" when Jesus was captured. It was just a little servant girl asking him. It wasn't a madman holding a knife at Peter's throat—just a little servant girl asking, "Hey, weren't you with this man Jesus?"

And Peter cursed and swore and said (in effect), "You're crazy! I've never even heard of the guy." He sinned (Luke 22:54-60).

Thomas the disciple was so dedicated to Jesus that one time when Jesus said, "I'm going to Jerusalem to die." Thomas said, "I'll go with You, Lord."

But there came a time when even Thomas doubted. After Christ's resurrection, he said "I'm not going to believe Jesus came back from the dead till I can put my fingers into the nail holes" (see John 20:25).

All of us, regardless of the face we wear on Sunday morning, regardless of how we can stick our chests out and say, "I'm a pretty good Christian"—we all stumble at times. We all disappoint God.

Falling Is Painful

What are the results of falling away from God?

The Bible says David was so torn up after the Holy Spirit convicted him that he cried, "I have sinned against the Lord," and went out and fasted and spent a whole night flat on the ground (2 Samuel 12:13-16, NASB).

Peter, after he denied Christ, turned and found Jesus looking straight into his eyes from across the courtyard where they stood. It wiped him out.

He went away and fell down on his hands and knees and the Bible says he "wept bitterly." It tore him apart (Luke 22:61-62, NASB).

And as for Thomas—after all his bold statements, when the risen Jesus walked into the room where the disciples met, Thomas said, "My Lord and my God!" (John 20:28) Think how he must have felt!

Remorse, regret, guilt and alienation—that's what happens in your life when you turn your back on God. I guarantee that if you knowingly reject God's way and go your own way, immediately you'll feel alienated from God. He'll seem a million miles away.

In fact, I'd venture to say you'll have a very hard time *praying.* You might even feel that you *can't* pray. I know I can't. I can't pretend that everything is fine when I know I've disappointed the Person I love most, the Person who loves me beyond words.

And then there's the guilt. Some people live a lifetime crippled by the weight of guilt, which tragically destroys their self-image. I've talked with people who think so little of themselves that they just don't care what happens.

What a difference between that kind of attitude and the kind of excitement God puts in your life when you're following Him and you know He's got great things in store for you!

But that's what sin does to you. Sin robs people of the most precious commodity in life—the sense of the presence of God. Sin robs people of the closest companionship in life, the friendship of Jesus Christ. The way you live can be radically changed if you sense the presence of Christ daily, moment by moment. But if you lose that close fellowship—the quality will drain right out of your life.

We were designed to live in communion with God. We were meant to live close to Him. But we're human and we stumble and fall away. So then what? How do we get back? How can we regain that close relationship with God?

Fortunately, the Bible tells us exactly how we can do that. God knows our weaknesses, so He has a perfect plan for helping us deal with the sin in our lives and restore our relationship with Him. Before we talk about that, however, let's discuss some of the *wrong* ways of dealing with sin.

Games People Play

Though we hate to admit it, we all play destructive games now and then—even with God. These games are sad, desperate attempts to cover up the sin in our lives.

The first "game" to avoid is called *rationalization.* One way people rationalize is to say, "Well, you see, Lord—the reason I did that is because everybody's doing it. And since that's the case, I'm sure You don't mind *too* much." Sound familiar?

I remember I got a ticket for speeding one time on the Edens Expressway in Chicago. I was doing 75 in a 55 mile-an-hour zone. This was before the nationwide 55-mph limit and people were going 75 all around me—in fact, people were *passing* me!

Maybe it was because I had a GTO back then with big wheels and loud pipes, or maybe it was because I had out-of-state license plates, but for *some* reason a policeman ignored several other

speeding cars and pulled up behind *me*. He pulled
me over and said, "Let me see your license, sir."
He was very formal about it. He began writing up
the ticket and I asked him what I had done.

"You were going 75 in a 55-mile-an-hour zone,"
he replied.

"But there were people doing *80!*" I protested.
"They were passing me! I was in the flow of
traffic!"

He just looked at me. "Son, were you doing 75 in
a 55?" he asked.

"Yes."

"Then you were speeding," he said.

"Yes, I know," I said, "but what about all those
other people?"

"I'll ask you again," he answered. "Were *you*
doing 75 in a 55?"

"Yeah, but . . ." and then I got his point.

He looked at me and grinned. "I could have
chosen any of these people," he said, "but I chose
you." He said it like he had just awarded me a
fantastic prize in a sweepstakes, but I didn't find
his joke very funny.

Needless to say, I learned a lesson that day. It
doesn't make any difference what the rest of the
crowd is doing—if you know what *you're* doing is
wrong, that's all there is to it. Don't rationalize.

People come to me for help in ironing out serious marital problems. I usually take out my Bible
and read what God has to say in His Word about
how to have a successful marriage.

Many times their response is, "You've got to be
kidding. That book is 2,000 years old." They've
read the "sophisticated approach" of modern
psychology which says, "Vent your anger," and

they use that to rationalize their behavior. They refuse to accept the biblical command to be kind, gentle and tenderhearted.

These people continue, "Ah, we don't even know who *wrote* the Bible" (or some other excuse). "Psychology tells me I'm OK." And so they give themselves a way out—except that it isn't really a way out. They still have to face their anxiety and guilt.

So, *don't rationalize.* Don't play the game. When you commit a sin, be man enough or woman enough to say, "All right. I admit it. That was a sin. It's black and white." That's the beginning of the *real* way out.

The second game that people play involves *a flippant attitude about God's love.* This is a real favorite. People say, "Oops! I blew it but God will let it go by. He's an all-loving God, isn't He?"

Their concept of God is of Someone who's always saying, "Boys will be boys; girls will be girls; humans will be humans. Tsk Tsk." That sounds just great, but it's only half the story.

Oh yes, God *is* love. And God understands. But God is also *just.* God is perfectly just and He is holy. In the first letter of Peter, the Bible says, "You must be Holy, for I am Holy."

God is just. He's not going to snicker and say, "Oh well, you sinned, but I'll just forget about it." No way. If you're the type of person who plays around with sin—if you think, *Well, a sin here, a sin there, it doesn't matter,* you've got a big surprise coming to you.

You may be flippant but God is not. If you entertain thoughts of sin and then follow them through, you'll reap the reward—justice from a

Holy God. At that point, no matter how you try to cushion the impact by saying, "Oh, He's love," I would have to say to you, "Oh, but He's also *just*." And the tension between His love and His justice is something we all have to deal with.

So when you fall, don't rationalize. And don't be flippant about God's love.

The third game people play is self-crucifixion. And this is the one I'm really good at playing.

When I've sinned and turned my back on the Lord who loves me, when the Holy Spirit has warned me but I've followed my own path anyway, I later think something like this:

Oh no! God must hate me now. I'm a failure. I'm nothing. He can't use me anymore. He's going to turn His back on me forever. I'm useless, worthless. Why try? God's through with me now.

I crucify myself. My self-image takes a nose dive. My guilt becomes so heavy I can hardly bear it. I just wipe myself out.

Let me tell you how wrong that kind of attitude can be.

There was a time in my life when I fell away from the Lord badly, shamefully. And I felt God would never be able to use Bill Hybels again in any small way. I didn't know how to handle my failure. I didn't know how to get close to God.

Even after I read the Bible to see what God had to say about my dilemma, I still felt I had to crucify myself. Somehow *I* had to prove my sorrow by knocking my head against a wall and saying, "I'm sorry! I'm sorry! See how sorry I am, Lord? I'll crucify myself! See?"

During this period a friend came to me and said "We need somebody to lead a little Bible

study with a few kids in the community. Would
you consider . . ."

"Oh no," I said. "Not me. You know about me.
You know how I fell away from the Lord. I
couldn't."

And my friend said, "Bill, when are you going
to stop putting yourself on the cross? Don't you
remember? They crucified *Christ* so you wouldn't
have to go through this!"

He continued, "God can use you again, Bill.
Look at David. After David confessed his sin, God
forgave him, and later gave him a son who grew
up to be the great King Solomon.

"Look at Peter. After he denied Christ, God
used him again. He was the leader of the church
at Jerusalem.

"And Thomas. He went on to be one of the
crucial eleven Apostles who provided the leader-
ship of the first church. The same thing can happen to you, Bill. So quit crying. Quit crucifying
yourself. Ask for forgiveness and let God use you
again."

If it weren't for that little speech from a friend,
we wouldn't have the ministry we have today.
That small Bible study grew into the hundreds
and became Son City, a successful contemporary
youth ministry. Later we were able to start the
Willow Creek Community Church, a unique adult
ministry in the northwest suburbs of Chicago.
God has richly blessed us. Needless to say, I'm
glad I stopped playing the self-crucifixion game.

So don't rationalize. Don't be flippant with
God's love. And don't crucify yourself. Jesus
Christ was crucified for your sins and you can't
add anything to His perfect sacrifice.

Getting Back To God

Here's what to do instead, when you've got to get back to God.

First, *confess your sins to Him.* There's a very famous promise in the Bible. It says, "If we confess our sins, He is faithful and righteous to forgive us our sins and to cleanse us from all unrighteousness" (1 John 1:9, NASB).

If you confess your sins, God is faithful. He will forgive those sins. He'll erase them, blot them out. And then He'll wash you clean. He'll cleanse you so you can go on to live in His love and power.

What does it mean to *confess?*

When you confess a sin, you're saying first, "God, I agree with You. That was a sin. Your Holy Spirit has convicted me and I agree with You that what I did was wrong."

Secondly, you're admitting that *you chose that course of action.* Nobody forced you into it. You're no victim of circumstance. You have a free will. You can choose God's path, Harry's path, Mary's path—you can *choose.* Man is made in the image of God. Among other things, this means that man has a decision-making apparatus that he can employ of his own free will.

So admit that you *chose* the sin you're confessing. Sometimes it's really hard for me to do that. I say, "Yes, Lord, I agree that it was a sin, but *it snuck up on me,* Lord! I never really chose that." Then I have to stop myself and say, "Admit it, Bill. You chose that path."

That kind of admission exposes the darkness to light. The Bible says we should walk in the light. This means being really honest with God.

So admit your error and admit that you chose it.

Then thirdly, ask *for God's forgiveness*. Simply say, "Oh God, forgive me as You've promised You would. Forgive me." That's easy enough, isn't it? You don't have to do penance. You don't have to pay money. You don't have to get on your knees and hit your head against the bedboard to prove how sorry you are. God will forgive you if you ask Him to.

Fourthly and finally, *plan to forsake that particular sin forever*. Get rid of it!

I've found a method that helps me to do just that, especially with temptations that seem to plague me again and again. This might help you too.

I envision mentally that my life is a road and I've come to a fork. The road splits. So I say to myself, "OK, there's God's path on that side." (There's a big sign that says "God's Path.") The other path I envision has a big flashy sign on it that says, "Bill's path." I've learned in the past few years that God's path assures me of peace. I won't have inner turmoil on God's path. I won't be fighting with other people or with God. And God's path offers me the straightest possible route toward my full potential as a person.

Finally, God's path assures me that at the end of the road, Jesus Christ is standing with His arms outstretched, saying, "Well done, Bill. Well done. You've been faithful."

Now back to Bill's Path. I've learned some things about that over the years too. It can be expected to produce guilt. It will produce anxiety. It will guarantee a lack of the sense of the presence of God in my life. And it will hurt other people who are looking to me for help.

So here I am—at the crossroads—looking at the two paths. I know I have to take one road or the other. So I say to myself, "Bill, haven't you learned yet which path is the better one?"

If you can *learn to look ahead to the logical conclusion of God's way and of your way,* you'll find it much easier to choose the right path. Eve said, "Oh, that fruit looks good." She never looked at the consequences of disobeying God. She only looked at the temptation, and chose immediate gratification over the perfect life she could have had.

So when feelings of lust creep into your life, look at where they ultimately lead. When the urge to lie, to be bitter, to cheat, to vandalize— when *any* of these urges comes into your life try to line up the two roads in your mind and make your decision based on the consequences, not on the basis of immediate gratification or a temporary thrill.

If you want a temporary thrill, try backpacking or skydiving—get your thrills in legitimate ways. Don't string yourself out on passing fancies and cheap sensations. It's not worth it. It really isn't.

So what do you do when you fall?

Admit it to God. Get it out and admit it was a sin. *Confess.*

Admit that you chose the wrong path.

Ask for forgiveness.

Plan never to be a part of that sin again.

How Will God Respond?

What are the results of dealing with sin this way? Beautiful peace. Relief. A clean feeling that can't be duplicated or matched anywhere. The Bible says, "He has removed our sins as far away from us as the east is from the west" (Psalm 103:12, LB).

When we confess our sins, God takes them and puts them so far away that they can't be seen or felt. They're *just plain gone*. That's just the beginning of what God will do for you when you confess your sins to Him.

God also says, "Though your sins are . . . scarlet, they will be white as snow" (Isaiah 1:18, NASB). No matter how bloody red your sins may have been, no matter how far you've fallen, God can cleanse you. He can make your sins as white as snow. This means that your conscience will be free. There won't be that nagging feeling of guilt that you can't shake. You'll be perfectly clean, just like a country hillside after a fresh snowfall.

But God doesn't stop there. In the book of Jeremiah, God says in essence that He'll develop an instant case of amnesia about your sins. That's right, He'll forget what you've done. He says, "I will forgive and forget their sins" (Jeremiah 31:34, LB).

Do you ever worry about someday going to heaven and finding an overhead projector with your name off to the left and all your sins listed for everyone to see? It won't happen if you confess your sins. God doesn't keep a scorecard. He's not one who gets His kicks by counting up points against us. He wants to forgive us and throw the scorecard away and forget the past. But *we* need to get the guilt off *our* chests by confessing our sins to God.

There's nothing in this world like the reality and the feeling of coming clean with the Lord of the universe. And it's not an impossible goal; we *can* walk in the light. We *can* live with God's peace and forgiveness as an everyday reality. All it takes is the courage to admit our sins to God and ask for His forgiveness.

But is all of this "cleanness" and freedom an end in itself?

No. We're free for a purpose. God has given us this plan so that we won't get bogged down and hung up by the wrong things we've done. In the book of Philippians, Paul says that after we've confessed and God has forgiven us, we should put the past behind us and run full speed ahead toward what God has for us in the future (see Philippians 3:13-14).

You don't have to wallow in the mire. The Lord has made a way for you to put your past behind you and *press on*. Your whole life awaits you. God wants to do great things through you, and now you can be free to do them. My prayer is that you *will* press on.

Don't rationalize with your sins. Don't be flippant, and don't crucify yourself either. Instead, *agree* that your sin was a sin, *admit* that you chose the wrong path, and *ask God for His forgiveness*. He'll give it to you. Finally, plan to put that sin out of your life.

Then you'll feel the peace of God. You'll feel the arms of Jesus around you and He'll be saying, "It's OK now. It's done with. Put it behind you. Let's walk hand in hand through life."

7
How To
Be a Friend

A vertical, personal relationship with the God of the universe is at the heart of Christianity. But that's not all the Bible talks about. It also says a lot about our relationships with *people*.

It's not hard to see why God would help us in our horizontal relationships. We *need* help.

I know of people whose lives are devastated right now because they don't know one single person they can relate to in a meaningful way. Employers have gone hundreds of thousands of dollars into the red because they couldn't get along with their employees.

Uncounted marriages are made up of two people who are deeply in love with each other and yet can't work out their problems. Some couples spend huge sums of money on marriage counseling, but still their troubles drag on.

I've seen families where each individual has a meaningful relationship with Christ, and yet the family is torn apart because the members have never learned to relate to each other.

On the other hand, I've met families whose standard of living isn't very luxurious yet they enjoy a level of security and a sense of belonging that others would spend millions to buy—if these qualities could be purchased.

What is their "secret"? Why don't more people—especially Christians—get along with each other?

Many well-meaning "experts" are pushing all sorts of formulas for successful relationships. Unfortunately, the various formulas are often opposed to each other. Take the problem of anger, for instance.

One psychologist (with all the right credentials) says we should handle interpersonal frustrations by "getting things out in the open." *Confrontation* is the answer he prescribes.

Another equally qualified "expert" says problems should be worked out internally. "Take your frustrations and go beat on a pillow, if you have to, but don't confront."

Still another recommendation is to yell and scream and vent all anger, whatever the result.

Whom should we listen to? It's no wonder that one well-known writer said, "The last half of the twentieth century will be known as the age of interpersonal confusion."

Mixed into this kind of confusion is a whole stream of suggestions thrown at us by the world of advertising:

"Do you want friends? Wear these jeans!" or "Do you want to build a friendship with a certain person? Brush your teeth with this!" These are the messages that marketing experts are constantly selling.

Movie and television plots only add to the mess with the kinds of suggestions they hatch. These are what used to throw me for a loop. I'd see a hero on the screen who was very cocky and independent. He was the star of the show, even though he couldn't care less about the feelings of other people. Everybody liked him anyway. And in the theater everybody clapped for him.

So I'd think to myself, *Aha! If you want to really make it, be like that guy!* After all, things seemed to work out for him. So I'd try to be a little cockier, more independent.

But soon I would find my friends saying to me, "You know, Bill, we don't like you so much anymore. You used to be sort of normal, but now you're getting cocky and cold. We liked you better the other way." So much for the suggestions of Hollywood screenwriters.

Other prime sources of suggestions are the old everyday armchair quarterbacks—you know, the living room geniuses. Mothers tell their daughters, "Play hard to get. Make the guys come to you." Well, that's easy for Mom to say, but what if you haven't had a date in two years?

Or what about fathers who tell their sons, "Look, when you get a bad deal, punch 'em out! Don't take any stuff from anyone. Be a *man!*"

Everybody's telling everybody everything. There's no shortage of advice about dealing with other people. And yet the world is a hateful mess. Everywhere relationships are breaking down.

There Is An Answer

I'm so thankful that we've been delivered from this plight of human relativism, where all the answers are equally "valid" but so few of them work. God has given us the *truth,* the solid truth, in the Bible.

What does the Bible say about relationships? Plenty. And it's not just one more human psychology lesson. It's straight from the Creator of this product we call humanity.

If you're at all cynical about the validity of the Bible, let me give you a challenge. I dare you to *implement* the seven principles in this chapter. I'm a pragmatist, and I measure things by whether or not they *work*.

Of course the Bible is God's truth apart from experience, but it *works* too. The problem is that many people reject the biblical principles, without ever testing them.

The basic secret I've learned from the Bible is this: if you want friends, don't worry as much about how to win friends as *how to be a friend.* The rest will then fall into place.

The media and the psychologists and the armchair quarterbacks all take the shortcut route: What can I buy to win a friend? What can I do to impress this girl? And so on. It's all so cheap and so temporary. You can see right through the whole thing.

The biblical alternative is genuine: Learn to *be* a friend and you'll have friends.

So—how do I learn to be a friend?

Be Comfortable

The first clue is found in the book of Philippians: "Don't be selfish; don't live to make a good impression on others. Be humble, thinking of others as better than yourself" (Philippians 2:3, LB).

The Bible is telling us not to go the impression route. It's saying, "Be normal. Don't try to be more than you are. Be a person who is *comfortable* to be with."

Did you ever notice that people gravitate toward people who are comfortable to be with? Think over your list of people you like. You probably enjoy people who let you relax—the ones who don't compete with you and don't expect everything to be just perfect when they come to see you.

Such people are inevitably well-liked. But you can't be a comfortable person if:

1. *You're overly opinionated.* Recently I was with a group of men engaged in lively conversation. We were having a great time until we were joined by a certain man who has a vocal opinion about everything. First it was politics, then religion. Then it was horse-racing—everything.

It was unbelievable what his presence did to our happy group. He polarized us. He made us uneasy. The enjoyable lunch we were having was ruined.

2. *Next, you can't be comfortable to be with if you're too worried about your appearance.* I attended a pool party not long ago, where I noticed two distinct groups of people. One group was really enjoying the pool. They even got their hair wet. They enthusiastically used the diving board and the slide. They were having a great time.

Then there was another group. They just couldn't quite handle the pool because they feared their mascara might run or their hairdos might get mussed. The men worried that their stomachs were maybe an inch too big and they didn't want to be seen in a bathing suit because they didn't have physiques like Burt Reynolds.

But which group had the most fun? Not the ones who were obsessed by what kind of impression they'd make. They didn't have fun and they certainly didn't add to anyone else's fun. They were much too self-conscious to be comfortable.

3. *Finally, you can't be comfortable to be with if you act too holy.* It's sad, but true. Some people act so "spiritual" that when other people see them coming, they hide. "Oh oh. Here comes So-and-so," they say. "He'll probably want to pray or 'get heavy' with me."

Believe me, I think sharing your faith in Christ is necessary. But it is not God's will or God's mandate that you force a vocal witness into *every* situation. Sometimes it's more of a witness to shut up and *demonstrate* God's love. That's difficult for some of us who are living for Jesus Christ. Jesus means everything to me. I think about Him very often every day. I even dream about Him. And yet *sometimes* I can't talk about Him because *right then* it would alienate the person I'm trying to be friends with. And once that person is alienated, my chances of ever having a positive influence are seriously damaged.

So, be a person who is *comfortable* to be with; avoid being overly-opinionated, too self-conscious, or super spiritual.

Don't Be Negative

The second principle that will help you to be a friend is found in the same chapter: "In everything you do, stay away from complaining and arguing" (Philippians 2:14, LB).

The Apostle Paul is saying, "You know why some of you strike out in your personal relationships? Because you're *negative.* You complain, you argue, you gripe—you're so negative that no one wants to be near you."

An argumentative person, or a person who feels compelled to tell the world how miserable his life is, will never make it as a friend that others will be drawn to.

I'm not saying we should never express negative thoughts. In a marriage or any close relationship we should be free enough to share anything —no matter how negative it is. But we must remember that there are probably only a few people with whom we should be that open.

People sometimes come to me for counseling and they say something like this: "I don't have any friends." So I say, "Why do you think you don't have any friends?"

"Oh, I don't know," they say. "Nobody likes me. Everybody hates me. The world's against me. All those dumb people."

And I say to myself, "I'm liking you less and less and I've only known you for 30 seconds."

On the other hand, a person who can make the most out of situations is always in demand. We had a church softball team one season that lost a lot of games, but nobody got dejected because we had one player who wouldn't *let* us get dejected.

Whenever one of us made an error or struck out, he'd say, "Remember, friends, this is *fun!* Right? This is fun!" And he'd flash a million dollar smile. This guy single-handedly turned the whole team around. Unfortunately he didn't turn our scores around. But we did have fun.

A positive person generates a type of enthusiasm that's contagious. If you learn to keep your complaints to yourself, you'll have gone a long way toward becoming a person that other people will want to be with.

Be A Contributor

The third biblical answer to the question, "How can I be a friend?" is found in the book of 1 Thessalonians: "Dear brothers, warn those who are lazy; comfort those who are frightened; take tender care of those who are weak; and be patient with everyone" (5:14, LB).

In other words, Paul is saying, "Contribute."

This verse contains several specific suggestions in the area of how to be a contributor. First: "If you want to become a friend," Paul says, "have the courage to correct the people around you who are in error."

Do you have backbone enough to correct the people around you? Too many of us are so insecure in our relationships with each other that we don't dare risk a friendship by trying to correct one of our friends in love.

Sometimes it's just plain necessary. When one of your friends is engaging in something that you know to be unhealthy for him, you're going to have to make a choice.

Go to that person, put it right on the line, and say, "I care about you and I treasure our friendship. I know I'm not perfect myself, but it looks to me like you're headed for trouble."

You'll be amazed at his reaction. The Bible says that a fool will argue with you but that a wise person will thank you for correcting him. Your

77552

friend, if he is wise, will end up loving you more because you had the courage to try to help.

This particular verse in 1 Thessalonians also says, "Comfort those who are frightened; take tender care of those who are weak." In other words, *you* be the person who provides the lift.

A well-known Christian leader has a saying: "There are two types of people in life: *lifters and leaners*." You can live one way or the other; you can lean on other people most of the time or you can lift the spirits of those around you. What are you, a lifter or a leaner?

You'll never develop meaningful personal relationships if you're always a leaner. You'll never experience all the fulfillment that can come in a friendship unless you are a lifter—which means you take it upon yourself to encourage your friends every chance you get.

Lastly, in this verse, Paul writes, "Be patient with everyone." This is an almost self-explanatory part of being a friend.

All of us have friends who occasionally blow our minds by doing something dumb or destructive. Paul is telling us to have a little slack in our ropes for these people. My wife and I have a saying we throw back and forth: "Give me a little slack today, please." If you can learn to operate this way with your friends, there'll be enough flexibility for elbow room in your relationships.

This flexibility comes back to the biblical concept of *unconditional love*—the kind of love that God has for all of us. If you can love your friends with no strings attached, they'll be able to relax as they learn you're not going to condemn them every time they don't behave predictably.

77552

Be Sensitive

There's a fourth major part of becoming a friend: it's the ability to be a sensitive person.

A sensitive person is quick to notice people's needs. We should learn to be on the lookout for signs that our friends and acquaintances have needs or hurts that we can help with.

The Bible gives some great advice on this subject: "Rejoice with those who rejoice, and weep with those who weep" (Romans 12:15, NASB).

If you can tell that someone is having a bad day, the thing you *don't* want to do is to whack that person on the back and yell cheerily, "How's it goin'?"

But how can you learn to become a person who's sensitive to other people? First, watch for facial expressions. When I talk to people, I try to look right into their eyes; people always tell you things are fine, but you can usually see through a person's eyes and into his heart and find out how things *really* are.

Another hint is to watch people's reactions as you talk with them. If you're trying to build someone up by joking around with him, you need to catch on if he's not responding to you.

Sometimes we're too full of answers or just too full of talk to really evaluate whether our advice or encouragement is really getting through to the friend we're trying to help.

Be Honest

Point number five in becoming a friend: *honesty.* The most frequent cause of breakdowns in interpersonal relationships is lack of honesty.

When my wife found out she was pregnant with

our first baby, she wanted to enroll in childbirth classes and have me go through the whole experience with her.

This meant that for six weeks we would spend one night a week with a group of people talking about childbirth. I wasn't too excited. But I went.

At the first meeting, things were going along as well as could be expected when the leader asked all the *husbands* to lie down on the floor and pretend *they* were going through labor! The wives were supposed to help us. I've got to admit, my Christianity went out the window that night. They were saying, "Push, push, push!" and I was thinking, *Kill, kill, kill!*

After two weeks I had had it. I told my wife she'd have to go on alone, because I just couldn't take those classes. She broke into tears. "You don't understand why I need you to come to these classes," she cried. "I'm not trying to put you through something you don't enjoy. I'm just afraid to go through this alone. I really need you to be with me."

What a fool I'd been. I'd never picked that up. But on the other hand, *my wife hadn't leveled with me about her feelings*. She could have made up for my stupidity by letting me know earlier that she needed me. As it was, we spent two weeks in a needless state of tension.

Please don't think I haven't been guilty of the same kinds of mistakes too. I've covered up some feelings and paid for it in problems myself.

The point is this: the degree of meaning and joy in any relationship will correspond directly to the amount of honesty displayed. The Bible says that "iron sharpens iron; so one man sharpens another" (Proverbs 27:17, NASB).

If we'll commit ourselves to honesty, we will be rewarded not only with the joy of warm friendships, but also with the challenge and stimulation that comes when people aren't afraid to express their feelings and opinions openly.

Can You Be Trusted?

This quality leads directly to the sixth factor associated with becoming a friend—*confidentiality*. If you develop a reputation for being a public address system, if you can't keep things in confidence, then I would venture to say you'll be able to count your close friends on the fingers of one hand for the rest of your life.

The Bible says this about the matter: "Like a bad tooth and an unsteady foot is confidence in a faithless man in time of trouble" (Proverbs 25:19, NASB).

If someone shares a personal problem with you, one of the worst hurts you can inflict on that person is to betray his confidence in you. He may not get angry with you—at least not to your face. But you can be sure he'll never tell you anything important again.

This quality of confidentiality is an absolute must in developing your ability to be a friend.

Be Loyal

Finally, the seventh quality on becoming a friend is found in the Bible in 1 Corinthians 13:7: "If you love someone, you will be loyal to him no matter what the cost. You will always believe in him, always expect the best of him, and always stand your ground in defending him" (LB).

Loyalty means you believe in your friends. It means you will defend a friend. You won't let someone slander him while you're around. His occasional failures won't stop your loyalty—they shouldn't, anyway. We don't prove any loyalty by sticking with friends only as long as they're perfect. How many people could stick with any of us under those conditions?

Finally, in being loyal, don't be afraid to *tell* someone you're going to be loyal to him. Not just your boyfriend or girlfriend or spouse—I mean a friend. Have you ever tried it?

If you haven't, you've been robbed of a beautiful experience. Once when a friend of mine was on vacation, he sent me a postcard that said, "In describing our relationship . . . words would spoil it."

That card meant more to me than if he had given me a thousand dollars. It brought tears to my eyes. You can take a lot of hard knocks if you know you've got someone standing with you.

Try it sometime. Let a friend know that you're going to be loyal—that you're with him no matter what. See what it does for your relationship.

Let's do a quick review. We've said that the way to build relationships and have friends is to be a friend. If you can learn to do this, you'll find a whole new world of meaningful relationships.

There are seven biblical qualities that will make you a better friend, a person that people will respect and want to be around. They are:

1. Being a person who's *comfortable* to be with—hanging loose so that others around you can relax.

2. Being *positive*—not making a habit of com-

plaining and arguing.

3. Being a *contributor*—willing to correct or help your friends when they need you.

4. Being *sensitive*—learning to sense the moods of people around you and respond accordingly.

5. Being *honest*—not covering up your feelings but letting people know how you feel.

6. Being *confidential*—able to keep to yourself things that a friend might reveal to you.

7. Being *loyal*—willing to stand by a friend and defend him, even when he makes mistakes.

If you can put these principles to work in your life with the people you know, I can guarantee that you will find yourself enjoying the kind of fulfillment that psychologists say is almost impossible, the kind of happiness that Madison Avenue says you have to buy, and the kind of joy that the armchair geniuses would give their right arms for.

And best of all, you won't be alone.

8
Repairing Friendships

"Go play with your sister, stupid!"

"Get lost!"

"Brad, I don't want to go out with you anymore."

"Greg, I want to switch roommates."

"Sorry, Bob and I have plans for that evening."

These are the sounds of friendships breaking up. The phrases change as people grow into adulthood, but they still hurt. Sometimes the ones that hurt the most don't make any sound at all. You just don't hear from someone anymore.

It happens to all of us. It can happen even between the best of friends.

You can handle a breakdown like this in different ways. You can just pretend that everything's all right—try to go your own way and let the other person go his way. If you don't have to see each other very often, you can maintain superficially that all is well. You can hope that time will heal the wound.

But does time alone ever really heal relationships? I know it doesn't heal mine. If I'm having a problem with a friend, I fester and boil inside, and the longer I do it, the worse it gets.

Usually, if you just try to ignore the problem, it won't really go away. We're just not made that way. God has created us to live with other people—in *community*. We don't have the type of circuits inside that allow us simply to gloss over relationships that are in trouble. We run into red flashers and warning signals. I'm convinced that certain people get ulcers from trying to pretend that they don't care about broken relationships that are tearing them up inside.

You often hear certain people say, "I just can't get along with over-sensitive, melancholy types. I just let them go their way."

On the other hand, you'll hear more introverted types tell you that they can't stand to be around a forceful, extroverted person.

This kind of a write-off of another human being is a cop-out.

We all need to grow in our ability to relate to people who are unlike us, and we'll never have that kind of growth as we ditch every relationship that isn't going smoothly.

So it's not enough to just gloss over a broken relationship. And simply breaking off all uneasy friendships is really the coward's way out.

What *should* we do when an interpersonal relationship breaks down? Can we face up to one of the most difficult passages in all of the Bible?

The Bible has some parts that are pretty easy to take. I love those passages. It says that we can receive love and comfort and forgiveness from Jesus Christ. The Bible says we can have God's Holy Spirit right with us so we'll never have to be alone. These are great verses. I could read them all day.

But the Bible also contains some *difficult* verses, with principles that seem to go against our grain.

One of these tough verses is found in the Book of Matthew in the New Testament. Jesus says, "If a brother sins against you, go to him privately and confront him with his fault. If he listens and confesses it, you have won back a brother" (18:15, LB).

Jesus is saying "If you want to save a relationship that has gone sour, go privately to the person who has hurt you and talk it over with him. You may very well be able to work things out."

Does that sound difficult? Maybe not. But let me assure you it *is* difficult. Let's take apart this message from Jesus Christ, piece by piece.

Go to Him

The first part of the verse says simply, "Go to him." That can be one of the hardest endeavors of your life. "It wasn't *my* fault," you may say.

Jesus says, "*You* go to him."

"But I don't even know why it happened."

"Go to him."

"But I'm afraid. I could get *hurt*."

"Go to him."

Why does Jesus insist on this kind of confrontation? Because it's a biblical fact that a broken interpersonal relationship can be a barrier between you and a right relationship with God.

Jesus explains it this way: "If you are standing in the temple, offering a sacrifice to God, and suddenly remember that a friend has something against you, leave your sacrifice there beside the altar and go and apologize and be reconciled to him and then come and offer your sacrifice to God" (Matthew 5:23-24, LB).

This verse is referring to a situation where *you're* the one to blame, and Jesus says you shouldn't try to worship God until you've apologized to the person you've wronged.

Christ is saying, "If someone has a reason to be mad at you, don't even bother coming to church. Drop all of that and go clear up the problem between you and your friend."

But remember that Jesus also says to *go to the person who has sinned against you* and work out your differences (Matthew 18:15). Either way, God is telling us that *we can't let sour relationships ooze their disease into our souls.*

God is saying that for His people, right human relationships are a part of having a right relationship with Him. You can't have all kinds of spiteful feelings for another person and still carry on a vital relationship with God. If you've got messed-up friendships, and you're doing nothing to make them better, you can't possibly expect to grow spiritually.

Go to the person, the Bible says, and at least try to work things out.

Couples come to me with situations that are tragic. I usually talk to them one at a time—first the husband will tell me something like this: "My marriage isn't what it should be, and I want it to be better—but my wife doesn't care. She does everything she can to mess it up."

So I say to myself, "Wow. This poor guy. It must be terrible to have a wife like that. I can see why he's having a problem."

Then later on that week the wife will come to me with a story like this: "I really want my marriage to work, but my husband doesn't. We haven't been talking for a long time. He won't break the ice. I want to, but I'm afraid he'll just reject me and laugh at me."

So here we have two people who are in love with each other, who both desperately long for a reconciliation, but *neither party will go to the other*.

Step number one: *Take that first step*. It'll be true throughout your life. *Go to him*. Take a chance. *Sure* you could get rejected—God knows that. But go anyway, whether you've been at fault or the other person was at fault. Either way, *somebody* has to take the initiative, so God tells you not to wait for the other guy.

When you finally make your move, you'll probably be received more warmly than you think.

In Private

Let's go back to Jesus' words. "If a brother sins against you, go to him *privately . . .*"

If you've got a relationship to put back together, do it in private. If you've got a beef against somebody, don't tell your football coach or your best friend or your boss at work—*tell the person you've got the beef against*. And don't bring anyone else into the picture.

This is a lesson I have learned the hard way. I'm good friends with quite a few people, so sometimes a person will call me up to talk about a problem he might be having with someone we both know. So what did I do before? I used to try to play God.

I would call up person B and say, "You know,

Person A's been talking to me and he says . . .
What? Oh."

So then I call Person A back (the one who called
me in the first place) and say, "Person B is having
a problem with the way you're . . ."

So I used to get into these things, going back
and forth until pretty soon *I* was part of the problem too.

Bringing third or fourth parties into your differences with someone else causes nothing but
trouble. For example: Let's say your friend Joe
snubs you on the street. He was daydreaming
about some future heroic feat he was planning, so
he didn't really snub you—he didn't even *see* you,
but you don't know that.

So you get mad and tell another friend about it.
He thinks to himself, "I didn't know Joe was the
kind of guy who would do something like *that*."
His opinion of Joe is lowered. He doesn't trust Joe
like he used to.

But, of course, Joe can sense that change in this
other friend. But he doesn't know what's happening so he thinks the other guy is getting stuck
up—and so on.

The more people you bring into the picture, the
more people get caught up in the tension. Pretty
soon you have a Peyton Place. Everybody's tan-
gled up in everybody else's problems; rumors
begin to run wild; and the group tension mounts
toward the explosion level.

This happens in churches. It happens in business, athletics, and family life; it can happen in a
youth group too. Somebody has a problem about
the way the leader does things. So he tells Joe
Smith about it. Then Joe Smith tells Bob Schmoe

about it. Then Bob Schmoe tells John Doe and some other choice friends. Pretty soon a whole group or organization is convinced that *everybody's* unhappy.

And all this has happened because *one person* didn't go to the *one person* he had a beef with. Believe me, the names have been changed, but this is no fantasy. It happens all too often.

But it doesn't *have* to happen. Not long ago a 15-year-old girl came to my office to talk over a problem she was having with a friend.

"I'm not going to tell you who this person is," she said. "I need your help, but I don't want *you* to have a problem with my friend. It's *my* problem."

We could all use that attitude. If you've got a beef, go to that person in private. If you must talk about it with someone else, don't name names.

Be Humble

Step number two: *Be humble.* If you come across like you've got it all together and your friend is out to lunch, you'll never get to first base with him.

You can express your humility by how you act and also by what you say. You might say, "Look, I know I've done things that have upset you in the past. I know you've been pretty patient with me. I know that I blow it a lot."

Spill it

The third step in this repairing process is the most crucial. Jesus says, "If a brother sins against you, go to him privately and *confront him with his fault*" (Matthew 18:15, LB).

In other words, *spill it.* Get it out. Here are a

few guidelines on how to do this:

First of all, do it *gently*. If you go to a friend and blurt out, "I've got a problem with you! Sit down and I'll tell you what it is!" you might accidentally run your nose into a fist.

So don't get hasty about it. There's a saying for situations like this: "Gentleness precedes confrontation and gentleness follows confrontation." If you're dealing with a friend of yours, just politely ask him if you can have a talk. As you begin, you might say something like this:

"I want you to know something right off the bat. I value our friendship and I never want to lose you as a friend. In fact, the reason I've got to talk to you is *because* I value our friendship."

Now you've cushioned the blow. Remember, nobody likes being told he's wrong. If you neglect gentleness, if you go to another person telling him his life is messed up, if you start playing God —beware of his left jab, because it might catch you. And I'm not so sure it shouldn't.

Just resolve in your mind before you even start talking that you're not going to get mad or raise your voice. If you're not willing to be gentle and polite and forgiving, you might as well not say anything at all.

So first, you try to be gentle in your approach, then secondly you establish that you're talking with your friend as an *equal,* as someone who is also quite capable of making mistakes.

Then thirdly, *get to the point*.

Be straightforward. Once your friend is ready to listen, say something like, "I've got to talk with you about what's bothering me."

Then spill it. Don't hedge around. Don't leave

anything out, but completely clear the air.

Then finally, Jesus says that if you go to this person, if you do it privately, and if you get the problem out in the open, "If he listens and confesses it, you have won back a brother" (Matthew 18:15, LB).

As you get into discussion, you might find that the other person hates that particular action as much as you do. I once told a friend, "I'm sorry, but I just can't handle your forcefulness. You never talk gently. I can't handle the way you wipe people out when you talk to them."

I was expecting to hear a denial. Instead, my friend said, "I can't handle it either. Will you help me to change?"

Nine out of ten times, that's the kind of discussion you'll find if you follow Jesus' instructions about repairing friendships.

So be gentle, humble, and honest. Your friends will appreciate your frankness because they won't have to wonder how you may feel about things they do. They know you won't be going around with a hidden resentment.

So we've seen that barriers in relationships can be barriers to spiritual growth. And it's been shown that each Christian has a responsibility to try to set things right with people who have wronged him and with people he has wronged.

But what happens if you *do* go to a friend, do everything right, and *still* he turns you off? It can happen once in a while.

A verse in the book of Proverbs says, "When a man's ways are pleasing to the Lord, he makes even his enemies to be at peace with him" (Proverbs 16:7, NASB).

I stumbled onto this verse during a period in my life when a person was trying to destroy me with vicious rumors. Every time I tried to restore the situation, it just didn't work. I found this verse in Proverbs one day and desperately staked the whole situation on that promise.

I said, "Lord, help me. Help my ways to be pleasing to You, and I'll trust You to cause this person to be at peace with me."

Within a short period of time a phone call came. "I've been a fool," the voice on the phone said. "Will you forgive me?"

God had melted this person. God stepped in and worked out the problem that I couldn't handle myself.

This helps to illustrate how strongly God feels about this subject. *He wants us to be at peace with each other.* That's why Jesus gave us specific instructions on repairing relationships. That's why God has promised to help out when even our best efforts can't patch things up.

It's all for our sake, to make our lives happier and more harmonious with those around us. But then there's another dividend. When we can repair friendships and be at peace with each other, the world can see the love of Christ in the way we treat each other. And that makes God happy.

9
Why Worry?

Did you ever notice that every day you're practically forced to digest a steady diet of anxiety-producing information. If you read the newspapers or read magazines, if you listen to radio or watch television at all, it's bound to hit you.

The energy crisis, the world food crisis, inflation, wars, revolutions—an avalanche of fear-generating reports—threaten to engulf you if you pay any attention to the news media.

It's no wonder that people become ridden with anxiety. If you don't have any way to counteract this onslaught, you're in for trouble. Many people are walking around today with an enormous load of anxiety and pressure that is the result of living in our tense era.

The most often prescribed drug in America is used to treat hypertension. The second most often prescribed drug is for sleeping disorders—for people too wound up to go to sleep. Probably 50 to 70 percent of the counseling I do is with people who are having problems with anxiety.

In view of all this, let me tell you I'm glad to be a Christian. Why? Because Jesus Christ has laid down some principles that can help me keep calm and sane in the midst of madness. And they'll work for you too. You don't have to follow along with the world and let anxiety rule your life. If you're willing to take the Word of God seriously, you'll find that there's a better way.

Jesus doesn't pretend that you won't have problems and tensions, but He says *you don't have to be ruled by them.* He offers six "peace principles" in the sixth chapter of the Book of Matthew, that can transform your life if you'll put them into practice.

1. Decide What's Worth Worrying About

First, says Jesus, "Don't worry about *things*—food, drink, and clothes. For you already have life and a body—and they are far more important than what to eat and what to wear" (6:25, LB).

The Lord is saying, "Don't you people realize that there's more to life than food and clothes? You're all upset about these passing things, while you ignore the real issues in life!"

So the first "peace principle" Jesus gives us is this: *Decide for yourself what is worth worrying about.*

A couple of years ago, I got into a short conversation in an airport men's room. I talked for four or five minutes with a man and as I was leaving, he said, "OK pal, see you in hell!"

Here was a man who had told me how hard he worked to make life comfortable for his family, how he prided himself on his good job. He had addressed himself to these matters with all his might, but he hadn't even stopped to consider seriously the biggest issue in life. Heaven, hell, God—they were all a big joke to him.

He left me thinking, *Isn't it sad that people are like that?* People knock themselves out for food and clothing, for material success—while the biggest questions they can ask themselves are staring them in the face, *and these big questions go unanswered.*

It's as if life is a used car they're buying, and they're only concerned with its paint job. Everybody knows that if you're considering a car, you'd better start it up, listen to the motor, test the transmission, look at the tires, and take it for a spin, because the paint's going to wear off and get chipped in parking lots anyway. What matters is how trustworthy the car really is.

Yet people have a tendency to look at life's paint job—never asking how trustworthy their lifestyle really is.

Madison Avenue would like to have you think that if you don't have a Vegematic and a swimming pool and two weeks in Hawaii every year and new clothes and fancy cars, you're really missing out on life. But I have yet to meet anyone who derived inner peace from these things.

On the other hand, if you'll address yourself to the real issues and let Jesus Christ have control of your life—you'll find that God can give you a contentment that makes you look around and be thankful for what you have, rather than being anxious about how you can get more. In other words, Jesus Christ can put your values in perspective.

So what's worth worrying about in your life? Is

it new clothes? Power? Popularity? Status? How important are these things compared with your relationship to Jesus Christ?

2. Discover Your Worth

Jesus then says, "Look at the birds! They don't worry about what to eat—they don't need to sow or reap or store up food—for your heavenly Father feeds them. And you are far more valuable to Him than they are" (Matthew 6:26, LB).

"What are you worried about?" Jesus is asking. "If God takes care of all those tiny little birds, don't you think He'll take care of you, His children?" So the second "peace principle" is this: *Discover your worth.*

A friend told me about a "pet motel" he visited once. It was quite an exclusive place for only the most fortunate pets. Each room was carpeted, air conditioned, and decorated, with a picture of the guest's master on the wall.

The masters even sent cookies to their pets from Florida or Jamaica, along with cassette recordings telling them "Hello."

If one of those pets ever got upset or worried, you'd think he was crazy. You might try to tell him that he had it made, that there was nothing to fear. "Don't you see how much your master thinks of you?" you'd ask. "He wouldn't think of abandoning you, of leaving you without shelter and food and good care."

Well, Christ is telling us basically the same thing when He says, "Look at how well your Father takes care of the birds. Don't you know you're worth far more to Him than they are? He wouldn't think of abandoning His children."

We are well cared for. When we let pressures upset us, when we tense up with anxiety and worry—we need to rediscover our worth in God's eyes.

Jesus told His disciples there are two kinds of shepherds. One kind is just a hired hand. When danger comes, he'll desert the sheep. But Jesus calls Himself the Good Shepherd. He said, "The Good Shepherd lays down His life for the sheep" (John 10:11, NIV). That's how much we're worth to Jesus Christ. He laid down His life for us.

If you're a child of God, you may need to remind yourself, "Jesus is my Master, and He has all the resources of power and love imaginable. I'm His precious child, and being His child, I can give my worries and anxieties to Him. He'll take care of me."

3. Worrying Doesn't Help

Jesus' next comment on the subject of anxiety is a question: "Who of you by worrying can add a single hour to his life?" (Matthew 6:27, NIV)

Does worry change things? Jesus says "No." So the third "peace principle" is this: *Worrying doesn't help.*

My father is in the wholesale produce industry. One winter when a freeze hit Florida, I asked him if he wasn't awfully upset about the situation. I reminded him that the freeze would cause shortages and inflation and it could severely hurt the entire produce market.

"Bill," he said, "I learned a long time ago that there will be inflation with or without my sleepless nights. There will be unemployment whether or not my stomach's in knots about it. And sometimes it will freeze in Florida no matter how hard I worry."

He concluded, "It doesn't pay to worry. Worry doesn't change things; it just destroys people."

And he's right. I've seen it happen. A person becomes so tense, so filled with anxiety, that he chooses an escape route to try to deal with the tension. Then the real disintegration starts as guilt is added to anxiety. It becomes a downward spiral from which there is no exit.

God's children were never meant to live that way. The Apostle Paul says, "God hath not given us the spirit of fear; but of power, and of love, and of a sound mind" (2 Timothy 1:7, KJV).

Paul is saying that you don't have to accept a life of fear and anxiety. God can help you live in self-control and power and love.

As a Christian, you don't have to be wiped out by every problem on the horizon. Perhaps the greatest testimony a Christian can have is the ability not to be decked by every obstacle that comes his way. People notice whether or not you're really at peace, and you can be. Jesus wants to make His peace available to you to heal your deepest anxieties.

You may feel that you have to pay a little debt of worry before you can give your problems to God. That's not true. When you realize how destructive and futile worrying is, you need to make a commitment to Jesus Christ and give your anxieties to Him.

4. God Knows Your Needs

"Don't worry at all about having enough food and clothing," Jesus says. "Your heavenly Father already knows perfectly well that you need them" (Matthew 6:32, LB).

"Peace principle" number four, then, is this: *God knows your needs.*

Once I drove a borrowed foreign car from Las Vegas to Los Angeles. I had an important appointment to get to, and it couldn't be rescheduled. As I pulled into a gas station just outside Las Vegas to fill up for the trip, I noticed water leaking from the car. The attendant checked it and informed me the water was coming from a broken water pump.

Since the car was a foreign make, I would have to wait two days for a new pump. I asked if he thought I could put some water in and drive the 285 miles to L.A.

"You're crazy!" he said. "That's *desert* out there! And you'll have to stop every 15 minutes for water." But rather than wait two days, I took off, giving the attendant his laugh for the day. I couldn't miss that appointment.

As I passed a sign that read, "Next exit 35 miles," I began to realize what a step I had taken. That's a long drive on the desert when you're watching the temperature gauge. And after that 35 miles, I knew, came Death Valley.

So as I was driving along with one eye on the temperature gauge, I suddenly found myself doing what every Christian does from time to time—I *worried!* I got all tense inside. I began to tell God my problems.

"Do You see the mess I'm in, Lord?" I asked. "Or are You somewhere else solving another problem? Look at this temperature gauge! It's gonna go up, I just know it! Look at the *gauge!*"

I had been working on this subject of worry, so I grabbed my Bible and opened it up to this verse we're talking about, where Jesus says, "God knows your needs." Then I felt stupid. I'd been telling God my problems, but *He already knew all about them*. He saw the gauge. He knows everything there is to know about water pumps. He's especially concerned about water pumps in His children's cars.

Don't we often repeatedly complain to God about problems that He already sees? With His infinite nature, He's able to see and to help all of His children whenever they need Him. He can zero in on your individual problem, and handle it.

Since God knows our needs and problems, what are we supposed to do with them? The Apostle Peter tells us, "Cast all your anxiety on Him because He cares for you" (1 Peter 5:7, NIV). The solution is not just telling God the problem—it's in giving God the problem. If you've got a burden on your shoulders, Jesus wants you to bring it to Him and lay it down at His feet.

Somehow I was able to do that with that crippled little car in the middle of the desert. And I made it to Los Angeles on time with just two fill-ups of water.

God worked it out that in this situation I received His peace *and* a happy ending. But it was the peace I needed the most. Sometimes God doesn't grant happy endings, but He'll always give us a more important commodity—the peace to help us accept any circumstance.

5. Seek God's Kingdom First

The next saying of Jesus in this series is one of the

most beautiful verses in the Bible. After He mentions how most people run after food and clothing, Jesus says, "Seek first His kingdom and His righteousness; and all these other things shall be added to you" (Matthew 6:33, NASB).

So that's the fifth "peace principle"—*Seek God's kingdom first*—make that your goal, and He'll take care of the details of your life. This principle is one of the surest cures I know for the anxiety and tension that can plague all of us.

I'll never forget a pro football game I watched on television a few years ago. O. J. Simpson, Buffalo's great running back, got tackled right at the knees and everybody thought he'd be benched the rest of the game. He'd been hit hard and the announcers thought he'd probably torn some cartilage in his knee.

But Buffalo got into trouble in the fourth quarter. With about 70 yards to go for the winning touchdown, O. J. limped back onto the field. They gave him a handoff on his first play, and a big linebacker deliberately plowed right into his knees again. Simpson limped back to the huddle as the stadium erupted in outrage at this "cheap shot" tackle.

On the very next play, O. J. got through an opening in the line and broke free. The first 15 yards or so, he was limping noticeably. He was in pain. But as he began to get into the open, his limp diminished. Then he was running full tilt down the sideline toward the goal line, his attention riveted on that end zone, blowing the doors off everyone who tried to catch him.

As he broke into open field, you could almost see O. J. telling himself, *I don't care about the pain. I don't care about the cheap shot that guy gave me. I'm running full speed toward that goal line and the only thing in my mind is getting there.* When he got to the end zone, you couldn't see O. J.'s pain anymore—you just saw his grin.

When a person is committed irreversibly toward a goal, and he's heading for it with everything he's got, the incidentals don't make a big difference. Jesus is telling us, "When a person is full of anxiety and tension, one of the most therapeutic things he can do is to set his sights on the goal of God's kingdom and God's righteousness."

What does that mean? It means looking above your situation and recommitting yourself to God's goal for your life.

You don't have to wait for all of your problems to be solved before you can serve God and other people. Be a *lifter,* not a *leaner.* It's thrilling when I see people, who have their own hurts, extending themselves to others. They're saying, "My problems can wait. How can I help you?"

If you have problems and anxieties and tensions, the best thing you can do is to firm up your commitment to Jesus Christ and start looking for ways to serve Him and help others. You'll see both the large and small things in your life fall into place as you put His kingdom first, as you run forward to His goal.

6. Concentrate On Today's Problems

The sixth and final "peace principle" that Jesus gives us is this: *Concentrate on today's problems.*

Jesus said, "Don't be anxious about tomorrow. God will take care of your tomorrow too. Live one day at a time" (Matthew 6:34, LB).

I began to learn this principle when I was nine or ten years old. I used to work for my father loading and unloading fruit and vegetables.

One day I had five box cars full of 50-pound boxes of potatoes to unload. There were 2,000 boxes in each car—five cars—that's 10,000 50-pound boxes of potatoes!

My father couldn't spare anyone else to help me, so he just told me to get started on it. He must have seen that I felt overwhelmed, because he told me, "When you look at that line of cars, Bill, it *does* look impossible. *But you only have to unload those boxes one at a time.*"

So I kept telling myself that as I worked. Five days later, the 10,000 boxes were in the cooler and the job hadn't killed me. In fact, I felt a sense of accomplishment.

Don't stockpile your problems. It's easy to look off into next week or next month and see things coming up, and get wiped out thinking about all the work you've got to do.

But Jesus says, "Just worry about one day at a time. Wait till tomorrow to worry about tomorrow."

The Christian life is a long climb, with its moments of exhilaration and its times of hard work. Your whole life lies ahead of you and God wants to help you grow into the likeness of Jesus Christ. In the meantime, don't be overwhelmed by your shortcomings. Let God work on them one day at a time. That's the way to grow.

Review Of The Six "Peace Principles"

Here's a quick review of the six "peace principles"

given by Jesus in Matthew:

1. *Decide what's worth worrying about* (6:25).

2. *Discover your worth,* how precious you are in God's eyes (6:26).

3. Realize that *worrying doesn't help;* it can actually be harmful (6:27).

4. Be assured that *God knows your needs,* even before you tell Him (6:32). Our job is not *telling* God the problem, it's *giving* God the problem.

5. *Seek God's kingdom first,* making His righteousness your goal, and He'll take care of life's details (6:33).

6. *Concentrate on today's problems,* and wait till tomorrow to worry about tomorrow's problems (6:34).

I hope that this chapter has begun to show you how much God really cares about you, and how little you really have to worry about, if you belong to Jesus Christ.

10
Self-Confidence

Have you heard the story about the newly-promoted Army colonel who moved into a new and impressive office?

As the colonel sat happily behind his big desk on his first morning in the new office, an airman knocked on his door.

"Just a minute," cried the colonel in a burst of inspired energy. "My phone just rang before you knocked, airman!" He turned and picked up the phone.

"Hello? Oh yes, General! Yes, sir! Sure, I'll call the President this afternoon. No sir, I won't forget. Yes, sir." Then the colonel hung up and turned briskly around to the airman.

"Now then," he asked, "is there anything I can help you with?"

"Well, yes, sir," the airman replied. "I've come to hook up your phone."

Nearly everyone can identify with the person who attempts to cover up a lack of self-confidence by trying to make a big impression. Sometimes, like the colonel, you get caught. Sometimes you don't. It's a sad response to life either way.

There are two basic human reactions to a lack of self-confidence. One is this "obnoxious egotist's" reaction which tries its best to impress and overpower people. The other is the "withering worm" reaction, which takes an "I-can't-do-anything right" view of life.

Neither type is very much fun to live with. And yet all of us have some of these tendencies in our own lives. Why? Because of *our human inability to find a real source of self-confidence.*

Of course people continue to try. I'm amazed at how many successful, college educated people turn to *astrology* as a source of self-confidence. They check their horoscopes and look to a certain arrangement of stars to give them confidence in themselves for the next day or week or month.

It doesn't seem to matter to them that astrology is one of the least constructive, most primitive forms of religion. What counts is the feeling of self-confidence it gives them.

Other people believe that *performance* equals self-confidence. In other words, they believe that if they're really good at some endeavor, they'll gain enough self-confidence to help them find success in all the other pursuits of their lives.

This may be partly true, but it can also be ridiculous. For example, I play raquetball with a guy who is really an expert. When we first started playing, he steadily murdered me. But lately I can beat him every once in a while. The other day I beat him 21-17. It made me feel great. But can you see me going back to my office and meeting some new person and saying, "Hi there! I'm Bill

Hybels. Twenty-one seventeen! That's me! Great raquetball player!" Anyone would think I was nuts.

Sometimes I think that one reason our American society is so utterly competitive is that people are convinced that if they succeed in *something*—a career, a particular sport, etc.—they'll gain enough self-confidence to carry them through life.

But how many things do you have to be good at before self-confidence spills over into the rest of your life? Most of the time, it never really happens.

Still other people look to *position* as the ultimate answer to their lack of self-confidence. When you're in high school, you sometimes think that a spot on the starting lineup of some athletic team or a cheerleading position might give you more self-confidence. When you get older, it's the powerful positions in business and industry that you may aim at.

But can position alone really give a person self-confidence? If we are to believe Woodward and Bernstein, Richard Nixon—who then held the most powerful position in the nation—fell on his knees in his "final days" and pounded his fists on the floor in frustration when the pressure closed in on him. Even the highest position in the land was not enough to give him self-confidence as the Watergate scandal broke open. He was crushed.

Many of us get the idea that rock stars and other celebrities have positions that guarantee self-confidence. If that's true, why do so many of them have such severe emotional problems? Why do so many kill themselves?

A position in life, any position, will not ultimately provide you with the kind of universal self-confidence you need to find.

So if the source isn't astrology, if it isn't performance, if it isn't position, what is the ultimate source of self-confidence? Is there one?

I believe there is. Whatever real self-confidence I have has come from only one Source: God.

I know that God, the Father of the universe, is *my* Father, and that gives me self-confidence.

I know that Jesus of Nazareth, the Son of God, is my Saviour. He's my Forgiver, my Friend, and my Controller. And that gives me confidence.

I know that the Holy Spirit of God lives inside me, giving me power and victory in life. So God Himself is the ultimate Power Source when it comes to self-confidence. He loves you. And if you depend on Him, He will give you strength no matter what formation the stars are in. God will lift you up whether or not you're a great athlete or musician. He can give you a deep, warm, gentle self-confidence no matter how high or low your position in life.

How can you plug into this great Source of self-confidence? One way is to begin to trust His Word. Listen to what the Bible tells us:

"If God is on our side, who can ever be against us?" (Romans 8:31, LB)

"The Lord is my Light and my Salvation; whom shall I fear? When evil men come to destroy me, they will stumble and fall! Yes, though a mighty army marches against me, my heart shall know no fear! I am confident that God will save me!" (Psalm 27:1-3, LB)

"Though a thousand fall at my side, though ten thousand are dying around me, the evil will not touch me" (Psalm 91:7, LB).

"The Lord is my Helper and I am not afraid of anything that mere man can do to me" (Hebrews 13:6, LB).

These verses just begin to show the kind of overwhelming confidence we can have as we trust in God. It's not that we're counting on our own efforts or brilliance. It's a matter of trusting that *God is with us* in our efforts as He leads us through life.

God Himself is the Foundation of our self-confidence as Christians, and our faith in God can give us a deep self-confidence that is firmly rooted in Him.

If you're a Christian, think for a moment what God has done for you. The God of the universe looked down over billions of people and He saw you. He called you by name, He lifted you up and embraced you and forgave your sins. And He put His own Spirit within you.

Now He says to you, "Let's walk through life together, confidently. Let Me be your Source of confidence and strength. You'll never fail if your confidence is based in Me."

If you're not a Christian, if you don't have a relationship with Jesus Christ, you'll never know what real self-confidence is unless you turn to God and let Jesus be your Forgiver, your Friend, and your Controller. You'll never have a satisfying level of self-confidence until you're born again. It's as simple as that.

Once you've been born into the family of God, however, self-confidence doesn't come automatically. As you go through life and hard times hit you, you may begin to feel weak. You need a way to remind yourself of your Source of strength.

A good way to do this is by developing a *creed*. A creed can help you when things get tough. Christians too can get shaky, can be filled with fear, and can even revert to being withering worms or obnoxious egotists.

You can often keep this from happening by repeating certain phrases to yourself. These phrases can be verses of Scripture or just certain biblical truths expressed in your own words.

Here are some phrases that might help you:

"I am God's child." Just saying that can do something for you. Try saying it to yourself at school, at work, anytime you feel your confidence slipping away.

"I'm a member of God's family."

"God's Spirit dwells within me and gives me power."

"I'm a person for whom Jesus Christ died on the Cross. I am *someone*. You'd better believe it. God thought so." (I say this one to myself sometimes 20 times a day.)

Besides the impact that positive creeds can have on your life, you need to understand the impact that negative statements can have. *Never, never, never* let your self-confidence be eroded because of negative statements. If you catch yourself saying something like, "I can't do anything right," you need to reject that thought.

When you affirm a verbal attack on yourself, you begin to believe it. If you tell yourself often enough that you're a loser, you'll begin to *be* a loser, just because you've convinced yourself.

Instead of saying things like, "I'm worthless," or "I always mess things up," when you make a mistake in your life, you need to be saying, "I'm God's child. He'll help me do better through His Spirit within me."

It is destructive to attack yourself and to dwell on your weaknesses. You should *admit* your weaknesses, but then look to God and begin to remind yourself how much you're worth to Him and how faithful He is in helping all of us.

The only real Source of self-confidence is in a living relationship with Jesus Christ.

You can remind yourself of His love and keep yourself strong as you use a biblical creed, certain phrases that you can repeat to yourself throughout the day.

But if all this is so, how come there are so many timid Christians running around? How come it seems sometimes that Christians have just as many problems with self-confidence as everybody else?

Once you enter into a relationship with Jesus Christ, once you commit your life to Him, it does not mean that all your self-confidence problems are over. But the foundation is laid.

Now you need to build the house.

I'd like to offer you some practical, down-to-earth ways to build self-confidence in your own life.

Specify Your Abilities
I couldn't tell you how many people come into my office and tell me they're total failures. "I'm no good at anything," they say.

That is never true. God has given all of His

children certain gifts and abilities. What you need to do is to find out what your abilities are.

In the 12th chapter of the book of Romans, Paul says you should be careful not to think of yourself more highly than you ought. "Rather think of yourself with sober judgment," he says, "in accordance with the measure of faith God has given you" (12:3, NIV).

But in the statements following this verse, Paul makes it clear that *each Christian has certain spiritual gifts and abilities that can be used to help other Christians and to reach out to the world.* (See 12:4-8.)

Many Christians play a subtle trick on themselves with the concept of *humility*. They misunderstand what true humility is. It isn't humility that says, "I can't do anything."

Some people seem to think that the way to guarantee humility for themselves is to say, "Who *me?* I can't do anything. See how humble and modest I am?"

That's wrong. That's not humility. You should be unashamed to recognize the abilities that God has given you. God never made an Edsel. He never made a human being who was predestined to be a total failure. No matter who you are, I'll bet that if you and I sat down and talked for 20 minutes, we could come up with 5 or 10 talents that you have.

Recognizing your abilities is not pride. To think that you can use them without God's blessing is pride—but *to decide for yourself that you don't have any talents God could use is in itself a subtle form of pride.* And what's more, it can leave you with an awfully barren Christian life.

Your abilities don't have to be glamorous or earthshaking to be important. For example, you may say, "Oh, I'm not so special. I just want to be a housewife." Well, if you look at the Bible, you'll discover that God considers motherhood to be a precious and crucial task.

You might think you have to be a pastor or a singer, someone on the "front lines" of the Christian action, to be important. Not so. King David proclaimed that the people who held down the fort while his soldiers were away fighting were just as important as the brave soldiers themselves (1 Samuel 30:24).

With whom are you comparing yourself? Why should you feel bad because you can't play tennis like Jimmy Connors? Tennis is his *business*. It's all he does. It's not all you do. Should you quit singing because you can't sing like Beverly Sills? Maybe you can't, but that doesn't mean you can't be an asset to a music group of some type. It doesn't mean you shouldn't enjoy and use whatever talent God has given you.

As you're specifying your abilities, make sure that you *compare yourself with relative equals.* Not everybody can be a star. You can aim at excellence, but don't feel your abilities must be absolutely awesome before they can be used by God.

Watch out for your critics. Some people practically make a career out of deflating other people's confidence. Perhaps they're frustrated at their own lack of talent; sometimes they're just people with a negative outlook on life.

In any case, you should watch out for this type of person, and don't let negative reactions destroy your self-confidence.

I once had the opportunity to talk with Ken Taylor, the man who developed *The Living Bible.* During our conversation, I thanked him for his contribution to the cause of Jesus Christ.

"I know hundreds of people whose lives have been changed because of your work in putting the Bible into everyday language," I told him. (Of course there are millions more people, I'm sure, that I *don't* know about.)

He acknowledged my thanks and then said sadly, "You know, I've received unbelievable criticisms about *The Living Bible.*" I knew that. I had read some of the attacks—people bitterly upset because they felt Ken Taylor hadn't used just the right words in certain places. It didn't seem to matter to these critics that *The Living Bible* was communicating God's Word to a whole new audience of English-speaking people.

"I've been so bitterly attacked that sometimes I wonder if it's worth it at all," Mr. Taylor told me.

The Living Bible has sold over 20 million copies so far. It has reached into the world in a dramatic way, but still there are people chipping away at the self-confidence of Ken Taylor. God grant him the courage to continue doing what he believes is right anyway.

If you have a bright new idea and you get nothing but wet blankets thrown on it, make sure that your critics aren't just taking blind potshots. Think twice before you listen too closely.

Stretch Your Abilities

When I was very young, I was the timid type. Social situations were scary to me. I'm thankful that my parents recognized this problem and tried their best to give me lots of new activities to take part in as a child.

They *stretched my abilities* and helped me get over my problem. (Of course, my wife tells me I've got a worse problem now—of not being timid enough.)

Do you realize that if you never tried anything new, if you never ventured into areas where you're uneasy, *you'd never accomplish anything?* You'd be nothing but a human blob!

When Jesus sent out the first large group of what would later be called "missionaries," He told them, "I am sending you out like lambs among wolves" (Luke 10:3, NIV).

Sounds pretty frightening, doesn't it? Jesus was sending a relatively untrained "invasion force" into a world that often would not understand His message, into a world that could be cold and even hostile. But it was necessary that He send these people out, partly because it would build up their faith and self-confidence.

No doubt these early believers were apprehensive as they began their journey, but what happened? "The 70 returned with joy and said, 'Lord, even the demons submit to us in Your name'" (Luke 10:17, NIV).

So these early followers of Jesus were built up by a *test,* by stepping out into the unknown and *stretching their abilities.* The same principle can work in your life, if you trust Jesus Christ to help you.

Perhaps facing your biggest fear and tackling it with God would help you more than anything else. What is your biggest fear? Is it meeting new people? Public speaking? Trying some sport?

Whatever it is, if you'll grab onto it with God's help, I have a sneaking suspicion that you can beat it, that God can empower you to do what you don't think you can do. And if you succeed, your self-confidence will be built up.

But what if you fail? What have you lost? A little "face" perhaps. What have you gained? You may have at least learned one or two things that you'd never have learned without trying.

Not too long ago, I was seized by an urge to play the trombone. My neighbors suffered. My wife suffered. But I kept at it for a while. Finally I had to admit I wasn't going to be a trombone player. But now at least I know the basics about the trombone. I can read the bass clef. I know how to oil the slide. I can even recognize popular brand names of trombones. So, that experience was *not* total defeat, was it?

I've learned something. It didn't hurt me to fail. I don't regret it at all.

Sort Out Your Abilities

As you *specify your abilities,* your self-confidence will grow. As you *stretch your abilities,* you'll become proficient in many areas of life. But it is also very important that you *sort out your abilities.*

I made a reference earlier to the fact that my racketball skill, no matter how proud it makes me, is of little use in helping me be a better Christian leader.

Which of your abilities are really important? Which ones can God use in a significant way? For example, what difference does it make *in terms of eternity* if I'm a great raquetball player? None.

Jesus put it well when He approached Simon

Peter and his brother Andrew. They were busy at their work. They were fishermen—Jesus could see that. He could probably see that they were quite proficient fishermen, but what did He say?

"Follow Me, and I will make you fishers of men" (Matthew 4:19, NIV). He was saying, "I can see that you're experienced fishermen, but I'm asking you to do something more important."

So if you've become proficient in many areas of life, don't rest on your laurels. Find out what you can do for the kingdom of God—something that will last for eternity. Find out what your truly important abilities are, and then begin to exercise them in the power of God's Holy Spirit.

Then you can begin to be productive for Jesus Christ. Then you can reach out and help other people who are still secretly afraid inside.

There's a magnetism about people who have developed a godly self-confidence. People will look at you and wonder what your secret is. That's the time to say it unashamedly. Tell them who the Source of your self-confidence is. Shout from the mountaintops that Jesus Christ, the risen Son of God, is your Source of self-confidence, that your relationship with Him has given your life new power and peace.

Jesus said that basically there are two types of people on this earth. There are people who build their lives on foundations of sand—things such as astrology or performance or position or possessions. When the floods come and the winds blow, their lives are going to collapse. They won't stand a chance.

But on the other hand, there are people who build their lives on the rock-solid foundation of

Jesus Christ, on a born-again relationship with the Lord of the universe. When the storm comes, Jesus said, those lives will stand firm (see Matthew 7:24-27).

As you begin to build self-confidence in your life, *reach out to the Source of all godly self-confidence—Jesus Christ.* But first of all, be sure you are born again into His family.

Remember God's Word. It can help you remain firm in your confidence, especially the verses mentioned in this chapter. Try developing a *creed* of confidence—several phrases you can say to yourself during the day to remind yourself that God is with you.

Then begin to *specify your abilities,* to *stretch your abilities,* and to *sort out your abilities.*

God can't use you if you're convinced that you're useless. I hope you know that you're not. My prayer is that you'll stick your neck out a little and find out what an adventure life can be when you have the deep self-confidence that comes only from your Creator.

11
Faith
and Perseverance

Imagine yourself standing outside a high-walled garden in the middle of the desert. The sun is beating down on you, the sand is blowing into your eyes—yet inside that wall you know there are trees and springs of water and lush tropical plants.

You're exhausted from your unsuccessful attempts to climb over the wall. Your knees are scratched and your hands bloody.

Suddenly you see the outline of a door in the great wall. Then you notice something half-buried in the sand outside the door. It's a key!

Joyfully you pick up the key and begin looking—there it is! A keyhole in the door! You put the key carefully into the keyhole and turn it—and the door glides open in front of you. You've found your way into the garden, and it's even more beautiful than you imagined.

The kingdom of God is like that garden. There are lots of people who try to get in by climbing over the wall—by their own efforts. But Jesus

Christ called Himself the Door. He is the only Way into the garden (John 10:7). And the Bible tells us there is only one key to open that Door, the key of faith.

"God says He will accept us and acquit us—declare us 'not guilty'—if we *trust Jesus Christ* to take away our sins. And we can all be saved in this same way, by coming to Christ, no matter who we are or what we have been like" (Romans 3:22, LB).

So faith is the key to getting into the garden—into the kingdom of God—through Jesus Christ. But it doesn't stop there. The same key can be used to work miracles in your life after you're in the garden too.

I've seen so many miraculous changes, hundreds of miraculously transformed lives in the church I serve, and I can point to one common denominator—*faith*.

Families have been drawn back together, businesses brought from the edge of bankruptcy, empty lives given meaning and purpose—and all because people *began to suspect that God can be trusted*.

"If you have faith as small as a mustard seed," Jesus said, "you can say to this mulberry tree, 'Be uprooted and planted in the sea,' and it will obey you" (Luke 17:6, NIV).

Jesus is telling us that when we activate our faith, God goes to work. God has sworn again and again throughout the Bible that He will answer His children when they call upon Him in faith. He wants us to *trust* Him.

I can remember vividly how I learned to trust. Beginning when I was only four or five years old,

my dad used to take me on trips with him in a big
semi tractor-trailer rig. Whenever we'd stop at a
truck stop or when the trip was over, I'd crawl
over to his side of the cab and jump down.

My dad would stand down on the ground, seven
or eight feet below me, and say, "Jump, Bill!" I'd
take a little spring off that seat, give it a little
swan dive form, and drop down into my father's
arms.

I never worried about whether or not he would
catch me. He was my *dad!* He *loved* me. He provided for me, disciplined me, and taught me. The
farthest thing from my mind was the fear that one
day he'd step aside and let me splat on the ground
and say, "The joke's on you, pal!"

Do you know how I could have really hurt my
dad? By fearfully standing up in that cab and
saying, "Dad, I don't think you'll catch me." The
same is true with God. He has promised to take
care of us always, no matter how trying the circumstances. He has told us to trust Him beyond
the limits of social and material security. And if
we don't trust Him, if we settle for less than the
exciting life of faith God has for us, we hurt Him
deeply.

As it was pointed out earlier in this book, God
becomes frustrated with us when we refuse to
trust Him. When Moses brought the Israelites out
of Egypt and led them to Canaan, the Promised
Land, God performed many miracles to take care
of His people along the way. Yet when they got to
the Promised Land, the Israelites were afraid to
enter it.

"How long will these people despise Me?" God
asked Moses. "Will they *never* believe Me, even

after all the miracles I have done among them? I will disinherit them and destroy them with a plague" (Numbers 14:11-12, LB).

God was so frustrated with the faithlessness of Israel that He was ready to wipe them out. That's pretty powerful stuff. God wanted to kill off His own chosen people. Why? *Because they didn't trust Him.* They didn't have faith.

Moses begged God not to destroy His people. "Forgive us," he cried (Numbers 14:19). "Let the power of the Lord be great" (Numbers 14:17, NASB). In other words, Moses is asking God to make His loving-kindness so great and His forgiveness so complete that His sinful people will be freed once again to become His obedient children.

The Bible is filled with stories of people who trusted God and the "power of God was great" through them. Think of Joshua whose dramatic defeat of Jericho stunned Godless people into developing a healthy respect for God's power. And remember David, who when just a boy awed the entire Philistine nation by his daring and deadly attack on Goliath. These were people who allowed God to exemplify His power through them.

What about you? Your life's story isn't finished yet. Are you willing to step out and trust God? It won't be easy. It will take a lasting *decision* to begin a life of faith. But it's a decision that will revolutionize your life. God can "make His power great" through you. But it's your decision.

What God is teaching us through the story of the Israelites is that *faith is not optional.* It's necessary. The Bible says that "without faith it is impossible to please Him" (Hebrews 11:6a NASB). But that doesn't mean faith is a distasteful duty.

On the contrary, it's the key that unlocks all of God's treasure vaults for us.

The Apostle James tells us, "If any of you lacks wisdom, he should ask God . . . and it will be given to him. But when he asks, he must believe and not doubt" (James 1:5-6, NIV).

Jesus said, "All things are possible to him who believes" (Mark 9:23, NASB). Does this sound negative? Does this sound like faith is some disease you ought to shy away from? No! Faith can be the single most exciting ingredient in your life. And God wants you to have faith so that He can show how great He is through you and so that He can give you the desires of your heart.

There Are No "Superstars"

As you read the title to this chapter, you may have wondered why faith and perseverance were included in the same chapter. Well, it's not because we *had* to have 12 chapters. Thirteen would have been just fine. However, as you continue reading I think you'll realize that we can't realistically talk about faith without also emphasizing perseverance.

Faith isn't an easy thing. God does not necessarily respond to our faith with overnight miracles and by changing tough situations into beds of roses.

I've talked with many fulfilled and mature Christians—I always try to find out what their secret is—and invariably when I find a person who is truly mature in the Christian faith, I find a person who has not had an easy go of it in life.

I've learned that there are no superstars in this life. There is no such thing, really, as a great person. *There are just ordinary people who never give up.*

"Blessed is the man who perseveres under trial, because when he has stood the test, he will receive the victor's crown, the life God has promised to those who love Him" (James 1:12, NIV). That's the Apostle James talking about the quality of *perseverance* in the Christian life.

He also says, "Consider it pure joy, my brothers, whenever you face trials of many kinds, because you know that the testing of your faith develops perseverance. Perseverance must finish its work so that you may be mature and complete, not lacking anything" (1:2-4, NIV).

James is saying that when you develop a sense of *perseverance* in your life, you're on your way to becoming a complete person. You're becoming all that God wants you to be.

But the whole concept of perseverance runs contrary to our culture. There seems to be a mentality running rampant today which could be called the "presto syndrome." That is, the attitude which says, "If it doesn't come easy, forget it." It's heard in statements like these:

"I've got a little cold. I'm gonna stay home from school today."

"I don't like this job. I'm going to quit and collect unemployment."

"Things are getting a little tense in our marriage. Let's separate."

Do you see what I'm getting at? This is how many people think today. If things don't come easy, they take the escape route.

In contrast, let me tell you this: *Anything worth having in this life will require a tremendous amount of personal sacrifice.*

Sometimes people call me long distance to ask how we put together our youth ministry here at Son City in the northwestern suburbs of Chicago.

"We ate, drank, and slept Son City for three years," I tell them. "It took most of our personal time. We had few hobbies and took limited vacations. In short, we knocked ourselves out for this thing. That's our secret."

Usually people are taken aback when I explain this. They wanted three or four points to write down, a little "presto formula" for youth ministry. There isn't one.

"Blessed is the man who perseveres when things get tough," says James, "because God will reward him." If you want a life that's full of good things from God, it's going to cost you something. There'll be tough times. There'll be hard work. But it'll be more than worth it when your goal is accomplished, when God honors your vision and your hard work.

How Perseverance Helps You

This quality of perseverance will help you in four key areas of your life:

1. *You'll become the person God wants you to become.* That's what James is talking about when he says you'll be "complete." We all have certain qualities we need to develop in order to be the person God asks us to be. Many of these qualities—like self-control, sensitivity, and patience—are really hard to develop. That's why most people progress very slowly in these areas. When growing gets too tough or asks too much, they just quit. They lack the spirit of persever-

ance that would tell them to keep trying no matter how hard or discouraging it is—no matter what.

2. *Your interpersonal relationships will improve*. Friendships, marriages, work relationships all take effort to make them grow. Don't just give up on people if they disappoint you. Give them a second chance, a third chance—and you'll find yourself with friends you would have lost.

3. *Your prayer life will improve*. Jesus told a parable about a woman who kept asking a crusty old judge for justice until he gave it to her. "And will not God bring about justice for His chosen ones, who cry out to Him day and night?" asked the Lord (Luke 18:7, NIV).

Jesus was saying, "*Persevere* in prayer!" If you pray for something or someone and you don't get an answer right away, don't give up! Keep on talking to God! He won't ignore you.

4. *You can reach your goals and dreams*. If God has put a dream into your life, if He gives you a glimpse of what you could become or do, He'll surely help you get there, if you don't quit—if you *persevere*.

"Anyone who has faith in Me," Jesus said, "will do what I have been doing. He will do even greater things than these, because I am going to the Father" (John 14:12, NIV). That means we shouldn't be afraid of receiving a great dream or goal or vision from God.

Most of the great movements and organizations that have carried the Christian message through 2,000 years of history were started by one or two average people who had a great vision, a lot of faith, and the courage to reject the "presto" philosophy offered by their society.

The Apostle Paul, Martin Luther, and John Wesley were willing to sacrifice and work hard and *persevere* for the God-given dreams within them.

How to Build Perseverance

Let's say, you've committed yourself to Jesus Christ, and you feel your faith is strong. Now your whole life stretches out ahead of you and you're wondering, *How can I build up my own ability to persevere? Where do I start? What can I do to help me get through to the end?*

Here are some suggestions on how to do just that:

1. *Use Jesus as your model.* Jesus was the model of faith and perseverance for all of us. He wasn't given an easy job to do; His was the toughest assignment ever given to a person in the history of the world. He was to redeem mankind by coming to earth and living a perfect life and taking all kinds of undeserved abuse and eventually allowing Himself to be tortured and killed for crimes He didn't commit.

2. *Don't be afraid to make major decisions.* Your life should not be like a river. Rivers simply follow the path of least resistance. Human beings should consciously make decisions.

When Jesus came near the time for His final journey to Jerusalem and the Cross, the Bible says, "He resolutely set His face to go to Jerusalem" (Luke 9:51, NASB). Jesus made His *choice.* It certainly wasn't the path of least resistance, but He was willing to go through with it because of the worthiness of His goal (Hebrews 12:2).

Many people never make a major decision. Their lives are just a series of minor decisions. Consequently they have no sense of urgency about accomplishing their goals.

Any decision that is made without pain or risk or commitment will probably be pursued without passion.

But if God leads you to make a strong decision about where your life should go, then you'll find He also gives you a strong sense of perseverance in wanting to accomplish the goal that you've decided on.

3. *You'll need perseverance to overcome mental and emotional pressure.* Sometimes a job can seem just *too* big. An assignment can seem just *too* tough. It can put a tremendous amount of mental pressure on you. How can you fight it?

Here are a few things to remember:

You only have to work one day at a time. Don't let a month's worth or work overpower you. The Bible says, "Each day has enough trouble of its own" (Matt. 6:34, NASB). Keep your mind on your immediate tasks only. It won't help to worry about tomorrow's problems today.

There are worse jobs. Try to see the positive aspects of your task, no matter how unpleasant they appear at first. What can you learn from it? What will the long range benefits be? Will it somehow bring you closer to your ultimate God-given goal? If all this fails, simply remind yourself that there *really are* worse jobs. That thought kept me going the summer I sorted rotten potatoes 12 hours a day!

This job won't last forever. It's amazing how much you can endure if you realize you only have to endure it for a while. No matter how rough the road, you *will* come to the end of it if you just keep putting one foot in front of the other.

Again, remember that no one ever went through more mental and emotional pressure than Jesus. Here's an account from the night before He went to the cross:

"He walked away . . . and knelt down and prayed this prayer: 'Father, if You are willing, please take away this cup of horror from Me. But I want Your will, not Mine.' Then an angel from heaven appeared and strengthened Him, for He was in such agony of spirit that He broke into a sweat of blood, with great drops falling to the ground as He prayed more and more earnestly" (Luke 22:41-44, LB).

What got Jesus through this awful time of trial? He kept close to God. And God delivered Him and gave Him the strength to face His destiny.

4. *Remind yourself of your goal.* You not only need to do this when things are hard, but also when circumstances are making things too easy.

The Apostle Peter tells us, "Set your hope fully on the grace to be given you when Jesus Christ is revealed" (1 Peter 1:13, NIV).

Even Jesus remembered His goal and kept it in perspective. There was a time when a great wave of popular feeling surged up for Him, but "Jesus, knowing that they intended to come and make Him king by force, withdrew again into the hills by Himself" (John 6:15, NIV).

Jesus knew that an earthly kingship was the "presto" way of doing things. It wasn't the ultimate goal that God had given Him. There will be times like that for us too.

So let's review.

What is the key to the kingdom of God? *Faith*.

What is faith? It is simply a willingness to trust God. With faith, all things are possible. Without it, we can't even get started with God.

So believe God and everything will be easy going?

No. Living a life of Christian faith requires *perseverance*. There are no superstars, only ordinary people who don't give up. With this quality in your life, you can become the "complete person" God wants you to be and you can fulfill your God-given goals and dreams.

As you build perseverance into your life, look to Jesus as your ultimate Model. By staying close to God, He stuck it out through the toughest assignment anyone ever had.

12
God Is My Refuge

King David is one of the most dynamic characters in all of the Bible. He's a personal inspiration to me, but he's not just my private hero—he embodied some qualities that everyone can admire. Though he was far from perfect, David was the kind of person that a lot of people would like to *become,* but very few ever do.

David was an *intense* person. He was a perfectionist in the good sense of the word—that is, he didn't do things halfway.

David *wasn't afraid to make decisions.* If he came upon a situation that required decisive action, he would say, "Let's do it! Let the chips fall where they may, but let's get going."

He was a *passionate* person. When David was down, he lamented bitterly. When he felt the joy of the Lord, he rejoiced heartily.

The story of David's life excites me every time I read it. I find something new each time I go through it. Why? Because David spent most of his life radically sold out to God.

David wrote much of the poetry in the book of Psalms. These were songs meant to be spoken or sung to the music of a crude harp. They formed a personal diary of David's deepest feelings and show us that he was an extremely *sensitive* person.

One of these, Psalm 46, has a particular passage that seems to have been David's creed:

"God is our refuge and strength, a very present help in trouble" (46:1, NASB).

Many scholars agree that David was expressing something very personal here from his own life. David was saying, "God is my refuge and my strength. He's a proven Friend when I'm in trouble."

This creed of David's helps us understand him. When you read through the life of David, you can't help but be inspired toward greatness. David had his terrible faults. He had his sorry downfalls. But he always came back to God. In spite of his dismal failures, David strove to please and to serve his God in a way that puts him far above the "average guy" category. He inspires us to live life *radically* as Christians. He inspires us to *excel*.

You may have seen a lot of mediocre living done in the name of Christianity. And you know you don't want your life to be like that. You want your life to be *different* somehow, not just a ho-hum experience. If you honestly feel that way, you're not alone.

But how can we find this radical Christianity that energizes every part of our lives? How can we learn to be self-confident, secure, peace-filled Christians who have an exciting mission in life?

What was David's secret? If you study his life, you'll find one crucial difference between David's life and most of ours.

David Bounced Back

For most of us, life is a series of small forward spurts followed by giant steps backward. We take two or three steps forward or upward, then something comes along that completely floors us. It could be a cruel blow to the ego, a bad day at school or work, or an argument with a friend. Whatever it is, it pulls the rug right out from under us. We fall flat on our faces and we have to back up four or five steps before we can start again.

David probably had more major set-backs and greater disappointments than most of us will ever have, but he *always bounced back*.

If you read his story, you'll find that early in life, David had one best friend above all others—Jonathan. They were "blood brothers" (1 Samuel 18:1, LB). But Jonathan was killed in battle while still a young man. David lost his best friend (1 Samuel 31).

Later in life, David lost a baby son as God's punishment for his sin of adultery with Bathsheba (2 Samuel 12:18).

And years later, David's favorite son Absalom led a rebellion against his father and eventually was killed by David's soldiers. This was a terrible blow to David (2 Samuel 15-19).

So in his lifetime, David tragically lost his best friend, an infant son, and later his favorite son. Those are some good-sized disappointments. And yet David endured them. He didn't crack up or lose faith in God.

Why didn't he just throw in the towel? Why didn't he just run off and say, "I've had it! Life is too big a burden. Life is too cruel"?

We all have disappointments—at school or

work, in our friendships, our families—that make us tend to turn and run. What made David different from the rest of us was that he knew *where* to run. When he was in trouble, he ran to God. He ran to his *Refuge*.

Instead of running to the bottle or the racetrack or to drugs or even to his friends, David said, "I'll run to my Refuge, the God of Israel. He forms a place of safety for me, a place not made by human hands."

David wrote the most famous of all the Psalms, Psalm 23. Here he said. "You provide delicious food for me in the presence of my enemies" (23:5, LB).

What David was saying, in effect, was, "In the heat of the battle, when I'm surrounded by enemies and hassles, I run to You, Lord. And here's what You do: You set a table before me right there so I can take a lunch break."

David says it's just as if God stepped into the thick of the battle and shouted, "Everybody put your guns down! Don't fire anymore at My friend. Stop the bombing! Turn off your tanks! We're going to sit down and have a Big Mac. We're going to have a shake, a few fries, some apple pie . . . and we're just going to rest a while!"

That's the way it can be in our lives too. God wants to refresh us, to give us a chance to regroup and face our enemies with new strength— whether we're fighting against depression, circumstances, or even Satan himself.

David knew where to run. He ran to God, who sat him down, set a table for him and gave him a chance to relax, have a meal, and get his whole act together.

David Got Strength From God

Some people might wonder, "Is that all that Christians do? Just run and hide all the time? God is their refuge; that's fine. But you can't just spend your whole life in hiding."

And they're right. You shouldn't live life defensively. Life is resistive. Satan is resistive. Unless there is a certain amount of aggressiveness in the Christian life, it is not complete.

David didn't simply say, "God is my refuge," and stop there. He said, "God is my refuge and my *strength*." He was saying that he derived *power* from God. Here David means much more than just shelter from the storm. He's talking about God giving strength to go back *into* the storm and face it.

There was a time in David's career when he and his men returned from a campaign and found that an enemy army had plundered their home camp and kidnapped their families. David's men were so upset that they talked of killing him.

David was bitterly disappointed, but the Bible says he "strengthened himself in the Lord his God" (1 Samuel 30:6, NASB). He was able to carry on then, winning back the women and children and defeating that enemy army.

This pattern is repeated throughout Scripture. When Jesus Christ was in the Garden of Gethsemane the night before He was crucified, He called out to God, "Father, if You are willing, please take away this cup of horror from Me" (Luke 22:42, LB).

It was as if Jesus was saying, "Those nails are going to be real! It's going to be such agony! Can't You take it away, Father?"

Then, the Bible says, "An angel from heaven appeared and strengthened Him" (22:43, LB). In a short time, Jesus was ready to meet His destiny. He was rejuvenated, strengthened by God to walk into the cruelest kind of execution.

The Apostle Paul also received strength from God. He wrote in his last letter, "The first time I was brought before the judge (for preaching the Gospel) no one was there to help me. Everyone had run away" (2 Timothy 4:16, LB). All of Paul's friends in Rome had deserted him when the going got tough.

But, Paul said, *"The Lord stood with me* and gave me the opportunity to boldly preach a whole sermon for all the world to hear" (4:17, LB).

God is willing to strengthen us in this same way. He's ready to stand with us through the toughest trials of our lives.

Radical life-transforming Christianity can be a reality in our lives when we learn to derive strength from God. The difference between a radical Christian and an "average" Christian is that the average Christian gets wiped out by adverse circumstances, while the radical Christian runs to God and receives strength and encouragement to press on.

"How do I do that?" you may ask.

I believe you do it the way David did it. You go out away from people, get alone with God, and you talk with Him. You might say, "Lord, You're my refuge. I'm coming to You now because I have nowhere else to go. I know You're my refuge—now Lord, be my strength. Fill me with your strength."

He will. If you know Jesus Christ personally as

your Forgiver, your Friend, and your Controller, He'll never turn you away or let you down.

Tough situations are not really optional equipment in the Christian life; they're standard at no extra cost. If you're living for Jesus Christ, there will undoubtedly be times when the situation seems just too hard to handle. It's then that you must go to God, run to God, and let Him strengthen you.

God Was David's Friend

In another psalm, David says, "God is my stronghold; My God in His loving-kindness will meet me" (59:9-10, NASB). This helps to explain what David meant when he called God a "tested help in times of trouble" (46:1, LB).

This second part of David's creed, where he refers to God as a "tested help," presents God as a *personal Friend* to His children. David is saying, "God Himself has come to me and has helped me before; I know He'll keep on helping me."

Radical Christians understand that Christianity is not just a set of ethics; it's not just a philosophy—*it's a relationship with God.*

A refuge could be just some impersonal place of safety. Strength could conceivably come from some mystical inexplicable source. But to David, *refuge* meant being embraced and protected by the arms of God, a loving and concerned *Person*. *Strength* was supplied by the encouragement and counseling of his *personal Friend*.

David's whole life revolved around a *relationship,* a *friendship* with God.

That's why young David was so angry at Goliath, the Philistine giant. Goliath was challenging the Israeli army, telling them that their God was powerless. David "ran quickly toward the battle line to meet the Philistine" (1 Samuel 17:48, NASB). David *ran* out. He was passionately upset at Goliath for his insults toward God.

He was saying, in effect, "Don't you *ever* talk that way about the God of the universe, who has become a Friend to me. You'll see who's powerless! You're going to have Excedrin headache number 27 in about 30 seconds! And you deserve it!"

God's personal nature also caused David to be deeply concerned after he committed a sin. He didn't just say, "Oh well, chalk that one up to my lower nature. Tomorrow I'll do better." David knew that when we sin, we're hurting a *Person*.

It's not the same as a simple slip from a code of ethics. When I'm flying my plane and I make a mistake, I may think, "Uh oh. I just violated FAA number 94.4." But what's the FAA? It's just a set of ethical rules backed by an impersonal bureaucracy in Washington.

However, when we commit a sin against God, we hurt *Him*. We're thumbing our noses at a *Person*, a *Friend*, not just an impersonal code or a dry list of rules.

That's why when David was convicted of his sin, he cried out, "I admit my shameful deed—it haunts me day and night. It is against You and You alone I sinned and did this terrible thing" (Psalm 51:3-4, LB).

Just as David was deeply grieved by his son Absalom, so he was overjoyed with his victories. Again, this was partly because of God's personal nature. When young King David was celebrating once, he "danced before the Lord with all his might" (2 Samuel 6:14, LB). He was criticized for it, but he didn't care. *He was sharing a victory with his God.*

You can share that kind of victory too. You can make David's creed your creed and say with him, "God is my refuge and my strength. He's a proven Friend in times of trouble." You can prove God's critics and detractors wrong as you let Him be your personal Refuge and your personal Strength-giver.

When you allow God to work and share in your life, He shares your defeats and your victories too. Your Christian life will not be "average" anymore, because God will transform it.

"God is my refuge and my strength,
a proven Friend in times of trouble."
He's waiting to prove it.
To you!